"Just as we suspected, and with impeccable timing, we find in McKenna's *When God Laughs with Us*, evidence that God not only has, but encourages a bountiful sense of humor and offers a written respite for leaders who often take ourselves far too seriously. Thanks David for insight into yet another delightfully creative dimension of our Heavenly Father."

—**Sandra C. Gray**
President, Asbury University

"In sharing many lighthearted and humorous experiences, often directed at himself, David McKenna reveals how a person can keep balance and perspective while making important decisions."

—**Norman L. Edwards**
Seattle, Wasthington

"*When God Laughs with Us* highlights encounters, at once serious and funny, each with its opening and insight into a deeper reality of our life with God. Dave's capacity to peel back the veneer that encases so many leaders and prod us to look deeper into our soul so that we can bear the weight of leadership more lightly is provocative . . . You will enjoy the combination of personal and professional anecdotes and be drawn into reflecting on the intersection of your own personal and professional 'life lessons.' You'll love the book."

—**Gayle D. Beebe**
President, Westmont College

"Dave McKenna, always in for a good laugh, has the gift of seeing the funny side of just about anything. And the comedic comes through, inevitably, in any leadership setting, especially for college presidents working with students who think up the most astonishing ways to pull pranks and have fun. Read this delightful little volume and I promise you laughter, joy, and healing for the soul."

—**Donald Demaray**
Professor Emeritus of Preaching, Asbury Theological Seminary

"In *When God Laughs with Us*, David McKenna treats us to priceless moments of personal gaffes, awkward moments, cultural tensions and, at times, hilarious slapstick type situations which rival the Three Stooges. Whether it is being drenched in water before a speaking engagement or arriving at the pulpit of the wrong church, McKenna allows us to see that leadership can be fun when we learn to laugh at ourselves. Indeed, McKenna's humorous stories wonderfully remind us of the truth of Reinhold Niebuhr's quip that, 'Humor is the prelude to faith and laughter is the beginning of prayer.'"

—**Timothy C. Tennent**
President, Asbury Theological Seminary

"What a terrific and timely book. For all of us in leadership, without question we take ourselves too seriously, to our detriment, I might add, limiting our effectiveness as Christians and as leaders. Dave McKenna comes to the rescue. Out of his long and storied career, and as a skilled storyteller, he hammers home a wise insight: We've simply got to lighten up a bit. In story after story, we find Dave leading and modeling a way for us."

—**Philip W. Eaton**
President, Seattle Pacific University

"When you need a cup of coffee and a good humor break, take time to read *When God Laughs With Us*. Once again David L. McKenna has captured through his prolific pen those humorous times of life when God smiles with us. Through insightful life stories of wit and wisdom the Christian leader will find this book to be refreshingly restful to the soul."

—**Charles H. Webb**
President, Spring Arbor University

WHEN GOD LAUGHS WITH US

DAVID L. MCKENNA

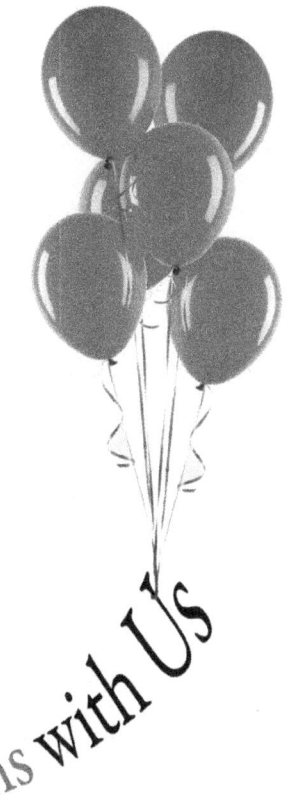

When God Laughs with Us

The Lighter Side of Leadership

CASCADE *Books* • Eugene, Oregon

WHEN GOD LAUGHS WITH US
The Lighter Side of Leadership

Copyright © 2011 David L. McKenna. All rights reserved. Except for brief quotations in critical publications or reviews, no part of this book may be reproduced in any manner without prior written permission from the publisher. Write: Permissions, Wipf and Stock Publishers, 199 W. 8th Ave., Suite 3, Eugene, OR 97401.

Cascade Books
An Imprint of Wipf and Stock Publishers
199 W. 8th Ave., Suite 3
Eugene, OR 97401

www.wipfandstock.com

ISBN 13: 978-1-60899-868-5

Cataloging-in-Publication data:

McKenna, David L. (David Loren), 1929–.

When God laughs with us : the lighter side of leadership / David L. McKenna.

viii + 128 p. ; 23 cm.

ISBN 13: 978-1-60899-868-5

1. Christian leadership. 2. Educational leadership. 3. Wit and humor. 4. Joking. I. Title.

BV652.1 M45 2011

Manufactured in the U.S.A.

Dedicated to the students of

Spring Arbor University
Seattle Pacific University
and
Asbury Theological Seminary

Who
never let me
take myself too seriously

Contents

Prologue: The Grace of God's Good Humor / 1

Chapter 1 The Apple That Fell on Plymouth Rock / 7
Chapter 2 The Prank That Rocked Western Culture / 11
Chapter 3 The Holy Hoop in the Sabbath Fog / 17
Chapter 4 The Dirty Spot on Clean Hands / 23
Chapter 5 The Bag That Let the Cat Out / 29
Chapter 6 The Tennis Racket That Unstrung a President / 33
Chapter 7 The Chapel with the Cha-Cha-Cha / 39
Chapter 8 The Untimely Twist of a Tangled Tongue / 43
Chapter 9 The Wet Finger on Ancient Crystal / 49
Chapter 10 The Buried Head on the Tilted Table / 53
Chapter 11 The Blind Sledder on an Alpine Run / 59
Chapter 12 The Jokester Who Should Have Succeeded Nixon / 65
Chapter 13 The Short Arm of the Law / 71
Chapter 14 The Rabbit That Played a Grand Piano / 77
Chapter 15 The Little Piggy That Went to Missions / 81

Chapter 16	The Yankee in Colonel Sanders' Court	/ 87
Chapter 17	The Rainstorm and the Rebel's Revenge	/ 93
Chapter 18	The Saintly Rider on a Wayward Horse	/ 97
Chapter 19	The Smart Campus That Sprung a Leak	/ 103
Chapter 20	The Ghost in the Choir Loft	/ 107
Chapter 21	The Bad Money in a Good Book	/ 113

Epilogue: The Joy of God's Good Pleasure / 121

About the Author / 127

Prologue

The Grace of God's Good Humor

> "There is . . . a time to laugh."
> —Ecclesiastes 3:4

SHORTLY AFTER I was elected President of Seattle Pacific College, our fourth grade daughter, Suzanne, came home from school after a civic lesson on U.S. Presidents. At the dinner table, she asked:

"Daddy, was President Kennedy great?"
"Yes, he was great."
"Was President Eisenhower great?"
"Yes, he was great also."
"Are all presidents great?"
"Yes, I think you can say that."
"Daddy, are you a president?"
"Yes, Sue, I am."
"Then why aren't you great?"

Our table exploded with laughter, especially from Sue's older brother, Doug, and sister, Debra. I tried to laugh with them, but like Macbeth's "Amen," it got stuck in my throat. I wanted my family to laugh with me, not at me.

College presidents are a very serious bunch. I first joined their ranks at the age of thirty-one when I was announced as the youngest in the nation. Because there is no exact training for the position, I began by imitating my presidential heroes under whom I had studied or for whom I worked.

My *spiritual* model was Dr. James F. Gregory, President of Spring Arbor Junior College during my freshman and sophomore years. President Gregory stood tall in my mind as the saintliest man I had ever known. His presence created in me an insatiable thirst for the Spirit of God. I took *every* course he offered, attended *every* speech he gave, and tried to get close to him in *any* way that I could. He still eluded me. My carefree spirit did not match his natural shyness or his Canadian discipline with its reserved response. I remember his measured smile, but I have no recollection of a hearty laugh.

My *intellectual* model was Harlan Hatcher, President of the University of Michigan. He and his wife, Ann, hosted Jan and me at a dinner in the President's Home after our appointment to the faculty at the Center for the Study of Higher Education. Our hosts and their table, featuring Cornish Hen, overwhelmed us with elegance and sophistication. President Hatcher remained in full control, telling stories with wide-ranging literary quotes, but still making us feel at home. There were plenty of smiles around the table and a chuckle or two, but never a laugh heard out loud.

My *executive* model was Novice Fawcett, President of Ohio State University, for whom I did special research while on the faculty. President Fawcett was the ultimate power broker, dealing with the faculty, handling the legislature, and controlling public higher education in the state. He allowed no nonsense in his Cabinet meetings, except when he talked OSU football and their arch rival, the University of Michigan. When I left the faculty at Ohio State to return to Michigan, President Fawcett announced my departure by saying, "McKenna is leaving for Ann Arbor College." The VPs waggled their fingers at me and scolded, "Shame, shame, shame." Then, it was right back to business.

When I first assumed the presidency, I tried to imitate my models. Pursuit of their spiritual, intellectual, and executive stature meant becoming very serious. I failed. To express the heart of my dilemma, I can only paraphrase an old quip, "I wanted to be a president, but cheerfulness kept creeping in." Perhaps it was my age. Because I looked younger than thirty-one, students kidded me about being one of them. The mask of seriousness didn't fit, so I decided to be myself, laughing heartily with the students and encouraging them to laugh heartily with me.

Still, I lived with my reservations. As a Christian, I labored under Nietszche's description of Jesus as the "grey Galilean." Did Jesus ever smile, laugh, or tell a joke? Elton Trueblood, one of my mentors, answered that question for me in his book *The Humor of Christ*. Defining a sense of humor as the ability to laugh at the ludicrous, Trueblood envisions Jesus with his tongue in his cheek as he uses the outrageous analogy of a camel going through the eye of a needle. Theologians who lack a sense of the ludicrous try to take the humor out of Christ's words. When they do, the message loses its meaning.

Norman Cousins, Editor of *Saturday Review*, threw me another lifeline in his book, *Anatomy of an Illness*. During a long hospitalization for a life-threatening illness, Cousins discovered the healing power of laughter. Imagine one of the most brilliant minds of the twentieth century getting better by "unquenchable" laughter as he watched old movies of the Marx Brothers. But, we never laugh alone. When two people share a sense of humor, they become what Cousins called "a Laughter Club." In fact, he found that some of the most serious-minded thinkers in history had also discovered the healing power of laughter—Sir Thomas Bacon, Immanuel Kant, Sigmund Freud, and Albert Schweitzer. I liked that company, decided to join the club, and laugh with those who laugh.

My dear friend and colleague Donald Demaray advanced the thoughts of Trueblood and Cousins in his book, *Laughter, Joy, and Healing*. As only Don can do, he gives biblical meaning to the therapeutic value of laughter by citing Proverbs 17:22: "A cheerful heart is a good medicine, but a downcast spirit dries up the bones." Then, he lifts the sound of laughter to spiritual heights in Paul's exuberant words, "Rejoice in the Lord always, again I will say, Rejoice!" (Phil 4:4). No further justification was needed for me to laugh as a college president. As a potent weapon against any uptight person who criticized my love for laughter, I could even quote Reinhold Niebuhr, who said, "Humor is the prelude to faith and laughter is the beginning of prayer."

All well and good, but my lessons in laughter were not complete. As a college president, I had to learn to laugh . . . at *myself*. This is the most difficult lesson of all because it means that I must temporarily drop the shield of self-protection for my presidential image, become fully human, and yes, even take the risk of being vulnerable.

We learn to laugh at ourselves when our flaws and foibles are exposed in humorous incidents. Norman Cousins said, "True humor is a sort of train wreck of the mind. You're going along a track and there's a sudden collapse of logic, the cars go off the track, and they pile up and build into laughter." Presidents and CEOs who look back upon their careers readily admit that they learned more from their failures than from their successes. Perhaps we also learn more from the train wrecks of good humor than by staying in the safety of the station.

I remember a silly slip of the tongue in a sermon that I gave before a large congregation. Building suspense in a story to tug at the hearts of my hearers, I was on a roll. Emotion gained intensity as I drove toward the climax of the story. Finally, with a weepy show of sentiment, I asked the people to imagine "a wounded war veteran entering the church and hobbling down the aisle on his *amputated* leg." People who caught the contradiction started a ripple of muffled laughter that spread in waves throughout the whole congregation. Still, I plodded on to a wimpish conclusion and a half-hearted benediction.

Afterwards, I beat myself unmercifully. Replaying the words and re-enacting the scene, I got a glimpse of my ego at work, manipulating the audience, exaggerating the facts, and playing on emotions. In the image of a veteran hobbling down the aisle on an amputated leg, the Spirit of God showed me "the ludicrous" in myself. He was laughing and he wanted me to laugh with him. When I did, I discovered the repertoire of God's great grace and good humor. He showed me my humanity, humbled me, and, most of all, saved me from myself.

I am now in my legacy years. At the age of eighty-one I identify with Charles Schultz who said, "In the game of life, I am living in overtime." Naturally, I ask, "Have I learned anything that I want to leave to the next generation?" Reflections on that question have already led me to publish *The Leader's*

Legacy: The Gift of Greater Things; *Stewards of a Sacred Trust: CEO Selection, Transition, and Development*; and, soon, a publication on incarnational sacrifice as the defining characteristic of Christ-centered leadership. Between writing these books of professional and spiritual legacy, I lifted the lid on the laughs and lessons Jan and I experienced together in fifteen years of retirement under the tongue-in-cheek title, *Retirement Is Not for Sissies*.

Now, I find myself joining with Charles Schultz when he wished, "If I were given the opportunity to present a gift to the next generation, it would be the ability of each individual to laugh at himself." For good reason, then, I chose *When God Laughs with Us: The Lighter Side of Leadership* as the title for this book. It goes beyond learning to laugh or even to laugh at ourselves. Please accept it as a gift that is wrapped in the great grace that God gives when he uses good humor to save us from ourselves.

David L. McKenna

Chapter 1

The Apple That Fell on Plymouth Rock

"Angels fly because they can take themselves lightly."

—G. K. Chesterton

"Let's all stand and sing, 'Amazing Grace.'" On that confident command, spoken at the age of twelve, my leadership career was launched—along with a lifetime of laughter.

What in the world was I doing, leading singing in church at the age of twelve? To catch the full humor of this defining moment, come back with me to the age of nine when I heard a sermon citing scriptural proof that children become accountable for their sins at the age of twelve. The evangelist used the story of Jesus being presented in the temple by his parents as proof of his point. As if quoting Scripture, he declared, "We do not become accountable for our sins until we reach the age of twelve." Great news for a hardened sinner who, although only nine years old, fronted for a teenage gang by putting eleven cents on the counter and lying to the storekeeper, "I'm getting these cigarettes for my uncle." (The storekeeper knew that my father didn't smoke.) This sin, however, paled against the time that I skipped out of fourth grade in the middle of the day and sneaked into the Wuerth Theater to watch Oliver and Hardy in Blockheads. At the age of nine I may not have been accountable, but I sure felt guilty as I sat in the balcony all alone with one eye watching the entrance for a truant officer. No wonder that I breathed a sigh of relief and decided to "sin boldly" for the next three years. On my twelfth birthday, however, the full weight of accumulated guilt hit me. I was a sinner doomed to die and in need of Christ's forgiveness.

Sure enough, in a Wednesday night prayer meeting where everyone had to testify or go to the altar, there was no escape. The countdown left me all alone with the option of faking my faith or confessing my sin. I stood up and blurted out, "I don't have a testimony. I am a sinner and I need Christ to forgive me." With a burst of tears, I ran to the sawhorse altar crying for mercy. My father came from the opposite side, met me at the front, and together, we "prayed through to victory."

My conversion set off a string of events. Of course, the prayers of my parents and grandparents were answered along with those of the little old ladies in the church who patted me on the head and said, "You are going to be our preacher boy." Most coincidental, however, was the appearance in town of another twelve-year-old boy who traveled across the country preaching at the county fairs. Billed as "Little David," the preaching prodigy and his troupe came to Ypsilanti, Michigan, in the same summer as my conversion. The pastor of our basement tabernacle by the railroad tracks must have sensed the competition and decided to put our own "Little David" on display. Starting at the lowest level of risk, he asked me to lead singing at the Wednesday night prayer meeting. Despite my age and lack of experience, to deny him was to deny God. So, I agreed to lead the singing of my favorite hymn, "Amazing Grace." Like all neophytes in their first leadership experience, I imitated song leaders whom I most admired. I remembered that they always smiled, asked the people to stand, called out the number in the songbook, and then told a story. Aha! As soon as I saw that "Amazing Grace" was written by Isaac Watts, my mind—the budding mind of a future history major—latched on to the story I would tell. Feeling extra smart before a congregation of God's best, but poorly educated, people, I spun my yarn: "Did you know that 'Amazing Grace' was written by Isaac Watts? He also discovered the Law of Gravity while sitting under an apple tree when an apple fell off and hit him on the head. This is one of the greatest discoveries in human history, but it is nothing compared to Isaac Watts' other discovery, when 'Amazing Grace' fell and saved a wretch like him. Let's sing it."

Wave after wave of gratitude rolled over the people. They sang, cried, and shouted as they sang,

Amazing grace,
How sweet the sound,
That saved a wretch like me.
I once was lost,
But now am found;
Was blind,
But now I see.

After five verses and repeats, I motioned for the congregation to be seated and left the platform in triumph to take my place in the old theater seats next to my grandmother. Because her approval meant everything to me, I waited for her pat on the hand and her good word. Instead, she sat motionless and silent for a moment or two. Then, she leaned over and whispered into my ear, "Isaac *Newton* discovered the law of gravity." All of the air went out of my punctured balloon. I slumped down in utter defeat. Little David had failed, and failed miserably.

While I demeaned myself and vowed never to lead anything ever again, Grandma came to my rescue. Bending down and whispering again, she said, "But no one else noticed." Together, we lowered our heads and laughed, not just then, but for years to come.

Only in the wildest stretch could we imagine what happened next. While I continued my "pity party" our pastor took his text from Genesis and the story of Abraham obeying God by "going out by faith, not knowing where he went." In a rampaging sermon propelled by "uhs" and "ahs" he pranced and danced on the platform in a one-man show acting out Christopher Columbus, like Abraham, sailing into the unknown in search for the new world. "Amens" and "Hallelujahs" took him to his peak when he shouted, "Praise God. Columbus sailed through storms that almost wrecked his little ship, but his faith was rewarded when he discovered America by landing on Plymouth Rock."

Grandma and grandson doubled over in a conspiracy of bottled laughter. Nothing was said until she leaned over one more time and whispered, "God is good."

Chapter 2

The Prank That Rocked Western Culture

> "Nothing shows a man's character
> more than what he laughs at."
>
> —Goethe

HUMILITY IS A leader's master teacher. Among the painful memories of my years in junior high school is that of hearing my social science teacher, Mr. Cushman, single me out with the indictment, "Mr. McKenna, you have a case of an 'exaggerated ego.'" I don't remember what provoked his comment, but I can still feel the sting. As a kid from the modest side of town and a member of a holiness tabernacle next to the railroad tracks, I cannot imagine any reason for having a puffed head, unless it was compensation for low self-esteem.

However it is explained, an exaggerated ego is not cured all at once, but by lumps along the way. One of those lumps came in my sophomore year in college when my roommate and I tried to be funny, but failed.

Homecoming at Spring Arbor Junior College doubled as Parent's Weekend. To show off the campus for alumni and parents, all of the dorms held open houses with prizes for the cleanest and most creative rooms. After talking over our plans, my roommate, Paul Hepler, and I decided that an open house was kid stuff that needed a touch of humor. So, tapping into Paul's skills as an art major, we decorated our room as an old-fashioned outhouse. The plan was that alumni and parents who opened the door would be greeted by a red carpet leading to a box fashioned as a "one-holer" complete with the amenity of a Sears catalog and a crescent-shaped cutout of a half moon shining overhead.

Our perverse creation never saw the light of day. Word leaked to the President's office and the order came back, "Lock the door and let no one in." Our aborted attempt at bathroom humor failed, one might say, on the launching pad. On Monday morning after Homecoming and Parent's Weekend, the Dean of Men knocked on our door and gave the order, "The President wants to see you, NOW."

All of the dread of parental punishment fell over me. My father never punished me physically, but I respected him so much that the look in his eye could spur me on, set me straight, or turn me around. Knots still form in my stomach when I think about the time that Dad invited me for a ride on Sunday afternoon. He didn't have to tell me why. He had trusted me with the family car when he and my mother went to Chicago for a weekend. By chance, on Saturday evening my father called home to let me know that they had cut short their trip and would be arriving early at the train station. He called to ask me to pick them up. Getting no answer at our house, Dad phoned the home of my best friend, Dick Peters. His father answered with a matter-of-fact tone, "Oh, they just left in your car for the movies." For Dick's family, movies were standard fare; for our family, they were a mortal sin.

Sure enough, as we rode out of the city on Sunday afternoon, Dad inquired, "Did you enjoy the movie last night?" Like a snared animal in a trap, I retaliated, "Yes, I did. How did you know?" Dad unraveled the story in keeping with my mother's favorite admonition, "Be sure your sins will find you out." At that moment, I wanted my father to beat me with a stick or ground me for weeks. Instead, he spoke simply and softly, "If you want to go to movies, that's your decision, but please don't use my car or my money." His words slashed me like a cat-o'-nine-tails. I had disappointed the man whom I esteemed above all others. Hell has no greater punishment.

So, as I headed for the President's office on orders from the Dean, the memory of that Sunday afternoon ride came back to me. President James F. Gregory had become my spiritual and intellectual father. He modeled for me the godly life and challenged me to go on and study for a PhD. Just as with my father, I knew that I had disappointed him by violating his trust. What would he say?

The President's secretary ushered me into his office. With tight lips and a crisp Canadian accent, the President stood, invited me to be seated, and came around his big desk to sit opposite to me, face to face. Dad's Sunday afternoon speech came back in the same tone with a different text:

"David," Dr. Gregory began, "There are certain proprieties in Western culture that we respect, whether we are Christians or not. Your display violated those proprieties. Bathroom jokes—whether in private or on public display—are *not* funny. You could be dismissed from college." He paused to let the truth sink in. "If, however, you can assure me that you have learned a lesson and something like this will never happen again, I will place you on the strictest probation. One misstep and you will be expelled."

No rebellion rose in me this time. As president of the sophomore class, I had violated my trust and disappointed my mentor. A foolish prank intended to get a laugh brought tears to my eyes as I asked his forgiveness.

From then on, I took every class in theology, philosophy, and preaching offered by the President, attended every speech or sermon that he gave, and led a non-violent student protest when the Board of Trustees asked for Dr. Gregory's resignation because he wasn't tough enough for the job. In fact, my next trip to the President's office came when I went in asked him to withdraw his resignation and stay with us. Again, the gentle voice of a lover rather than a fighter spoke to say, "David, thank you for your support. The decision has been made and it is time for me to move on." Within a short time, he was named as editor of *Light and Life* magazine, the official organ of the denomination, and served with great distinction as the spiritual and intellectual voice for the Free Methodist Church.

As my friend Paul Harvey would say, "Now for the rest of the story." When James F. Gregory died in the late 1950s, he had no idea that I would eventually follow in his footsteps as President of Spring Arbor College and then Chair of the Board of Trustees for Spring Arbor University. After I spoke at his memorial service, Mrs. Gregory told me that her husband had left some things for me in his will. We went together to their home and into Dr. Gregory's book-lined office. From the closet she pulled out his doctoral cap and gown and put them into my hands. Then, she went to his desk and picked up two books that lay there in waiting. One was a leather-bound, gilt-edged copy of Thomas à Kempis' *The Imitation of Christ*; the other was C. S. Lewis' autobiography, *Surprised by Joy*. What a heritage for a Tabernacle kid who could have been dismissed! The Gregorys had no children of their own, but they had adopted me. Even though the doctoral gown was a bit short, I wore it with pride for years and then passed it on to Doug, our oldest son, who still wears it today. *The Imitation of Christ* is on my desk for periodic reading of the best of Christian spirituality and *Surprised by Joy* is the centerpiece for my C. S. Lewis collection.

An aborted laugh that violated the proprieties of Western culture taught me how Christian leaders are like fathers. Showing unconditional love, they hold us accountable without crushing our confidence or losing faith in our potential. Any leader who says, "I am accountable only to God" is speeding on a collision course toward a total wreck.

Chapter 3

The Holy Hoop in the Sabbath Fog

"Laughter is the corrective force that keeps us
from becoming cranks."

—Henri Bergson

COLLEGE PRESIDENTS LIVE in a fishbowl. The public eye watches every move and passes judgment upon the style and stroke of the swimmer. The size and shape of the fishbowl itself may be forgotten. College presidents, as with all of us, have to live within limits, but their glass walls are narrowed by the expectations of their constituents and their culture.

The size and shape of the fishbowl for my first presidency left little room for me to swim free. As the leader of a conservative campus and a member of a conservative church in the 1960s, I had to watch my personal moves as well as those of my family. A psychiatrist would have a field day deciphering the effect of those limits on my presidency. Very early in life, and under the threat of eternal damnation, I had learned not to risk a fling at what we called the "Fundy Sins" of religious Fundamentalism—dancing, drinking, movies, and card-playing. On top of that, I had my teenage years restricted from such Sabbath violations as playing games, reading the Sunday paper, buying an ice cream cone, building a model airplane, or even listening to radio mysteries. Instead, my Sabbath days were consumed by Sunday School, morning worship, family dinner, and a ride in the country before heading out to the evening youth group and an interminable evangelistic service. At school on Monday morning, I felt deprived in the conversation as I heard my buddies tell of their weekend adventures—a dance, a swim, a movie, a model airplane meet, or a recap of Sunday night radio mysteries, such as *The Shadow*. My only compensation came when I learned to hide a small, portable radio under the covers, bury my head, and be brought to rapt attention by the sinister sound, "Who knows what evil lies in the heart of man? Only the Shadow knows."

Good humor caught up with my Sabbath rules when Jan and I were dating. While I could study on Sunday, but not play games, she could play games, but not study. We had a vigorous debate over the difference and finally agreed on a compromise. When we married and had children they could both study and play games. Still, I held tight on the position that playing games did not include attendance or participation in public sporting events on Sunday. Douglas and Debra, our two older children, have never quite forgiven me for denying them the privilege of swimming in the community pool on Sunday afternoon when we lived in Columbus, Ohio, and I served on the faculty of Ohio State University. Lifetime habits, especially when they are packaged as decisions on spiritual destiny, are difficult to break.

My personal beliefs about sports on the Sabbath were reinforced when I was elected President of Spring Arbor Junior College in 1961. A small, tightly knit community that centered around the college and church drew strict limits on the size of our fishbowl. The college gym, running track, basketball hoops, and tennis courts all witnessed to our respect for the Sabbath Day by being empty and silent. My position as President of the college and Jan's background as the daughter of the college pastor pulled the lines even tighter. Our children were expected to lead the way by attending every church service and being consistent models for the spoken and unspoken rules of the Sabbath Day.

Our little fishbowl showed its size on Douglas' twelfth birthday. As a budding basketball player, he had the dream of a full-size basketball hoop in the turnaround at the front of the house. Because I specialize in surprises, I carefully worked out all of the details for a hoop to be erected in the turnaround on the day of his birthday while he was in school. My schedule called for me to be in Chicago for a meeting on that day, but I exited early so that I could drive home at breakneck speed, paint a large sign for the back of the hoop with the words, "HAPPY BIRTHDAY, DOUGLAS." Everything went exactly as planned. At precisely 3:30 p.m. the school bus pulled up in front of the house with the faces of every kid pressed against the window as they saw the hoop and the sign. When the door opened, Doug flew off the steps already on the run and raced up the driveway shouting his happiness. Simultaneously, we stepped outdoors singing, "Happy Birthday Doug," and joined him at the base of the hoop.

Only one thing spoiled our perfect birthday party. Because the concrete at the base was still fresh, I had to tell Doug that he could not shoot baskets for another 24 or more hours. A brief cloud passed over his face, but he was so delighted with the gift that he quickly agreed to wait until I gave him the word. Saturday came and went as we checked the cement from time to time. Finally, we had to give up on the thought that he could shoot some hoops before he went to bed. Neither of us remembered that the next day was Sunday when the unspoken law of the community would be tested.

Doug and I went out early the next morning to test the concrete. As you have already surmised, it was dry and ready for action. But I felt compelled to say to my son, "You'll have to wait until tomorrow to shoot baskets. Everyone in town would see you." Saturday's cloud became Sunday's storm on Doug's face as he protested my decision. "What's wrong with shooting a basket or two on Sunday?" he demanded. I forget the explanation that I tried to give, but I suspect that it came down to the question of my superior understanding of the circumstances or perhaps (I hope not) a declaration of my final authority as his father. Whatever the case, no baskets were shot on Sunday, although I do remember looking out the kitchen window and seeing Doug looking up at the basket and mimicking a dribble.

My son rescued me from stress and shame the next morning. Doug, always an early riser, awakened me with the sound of a bouncing basketball at 6:00 a.m. When I heard the sound, I went again to the kitchen window and looked out. Heavy ground fog blurred my vision and created an ethereal scene that might have come from the introduction to the TV show *Touched by an Angel*. In and out of the mist I saw the figure of a boy dribbling on the driveway and shooting lay-ups at the basket.

Doug survived the moment better than I did. While I grappled with the shame of putting our son through the gauntlet of our public image and cultural expectations, he moved on. With the resilience of the young, he became the captain of the high school basketball team, with a deadly shot from the same distance as the outer rim of the turnaround. Seven years later we moved from Spring Arbor College to Seattle Pacific College. With the cross-country move, we were transported from one fish bowl to another. In Seattle, the fishbowl had expanded walls with more freedom to swim. I had a dip in that larger fish bowl two years earlier when I preached at the Seattle First Free Methodist Church in the Sunday morning service and attended a concert of the U.S. Navy Band as guest of the pastor that evening. To think of spending a Sunday evening without a church service and enjoying a band concert on a paid ticket, I had changed worlds.

I was not surprised, then, by the sight that greeted me on the first Sunday afternoon after we moved from Spring Arbor College to Seattle Pacific College in 1968. Looking out the huge picture windows of Hillford House, the President's home, I saw Doug shooting hoops with his newfound friends, Dale Foreman, son of the Academic Dean, and John Glancy, son of a prominent church member. I laughed at our newfound freedom in a bigger fishbowl.

Were we winners or losers? I still find myself resisting the temptation to make the Sabbath just like any other day for shopping and sporting events. The more I read Scripture, the more I realize that the Fourth Commandment is tied directly to the creation story and reinforced time and time again by research on the human cycle of work, play, rest, and worship. A healthy respect for the Fourth Commandment has never been cancelled.

As for the rigid regulations of the past, I might have become bitter and lost our son. But no, this is not the case. Whenever Doug and I want to liven a party, we tell the story about "The Holy Hoop in the Sabbath Fog." Invariably, it provokes a hearty laugh and a playful jab. Within the laugh, there is a lesson. We all swim in fishbowls limited by glass walls. No one swims free. The choice is ours. To gain the benefits of leadership or membership in a community, we also accept the limits. Change comes slowly and nothing is accomplished by banging our head up against the glass and bloodying our nose. Whether we are leaders or followers, the decision belongs to us: *Choose your fishbowl.*

Chapter 4

The Dirty Spot on Clean Hands

> "Humor is the reminder that no matter how high the throne one sits on, one sits on one's bottom."
>
> —Taki

BEING THE DEAN of Men on a junior college campus is like a boot camp for the presidency. When the setting is a small Christian school fenced in by rules, you have to be watchdog and warden, counselor and confessor, doctor and disciplinarian. The tensions among retention, rehabilitation, and redemption never go away.

At the age of twenty-four I took on this weighty role. To complicate the picture, I also had to be the Dean of Men for a four-year Christian academy that was still connected to the junior college. Consequently, my responsibilities ranged from ninth-grade brats whose parents could not discipline them to worldly-wise military veterans who came back to school in their middle and late twenties to take advantage of the GI Bill. At least two classes of students had been there as freshmen and sophomores in the academy when I had been there as a junior college student. Even though I brought with me the credentials of a bachelor's and master's degree, they stumbled over the title of "Dean McKenna" rather than just plain "Dave."

Recollections of those first two years of my academic career include incidents such as:

- Listening to "Heart and Soul" played incessantly in the game room under our apartment;
- Checking "Lights Out" at 10:30 p.m. with an eye for cheaters who stuffed rugs under the door to block out the light;
- Monitoring the probation of a young man whose prank had caused his roommate to jump out of the second-story window in the dorm and break both feet;
- Counseling the only African-American man on campus who was being stalked by a love-starved Caucasian girl;
- Confronting an older Navy veteran who was dating my sister (a college sophomore in the school); and even,
- Assisting the police when a murderer tromped through the dorm with muddy boots in an attempt to lose his pursuers.

None of these adventures, however, compare with the laughable lesson that I learned as an amateur sleuth tracking down a serial kleptomaniac who stole from fellow students time and time again.

The Dirty Spot on Clean Hands   25

Cash kept disappearing from student rooms on every floor of the dorm. Drawers were rifled whenever someone left the door unlocked for a trip to the bathroom. Warnings went out and precautions were taken, but the stealing did not stop. I decided to take the matter into my own hands. At first, we recorded the serial numbers on the bills and placed them at tempting places in drawers and on desks. The bills disappeared, but checks in the snack bar and bookstore produced no results. So, I resorted to the trick of sprinkling some invisible powder on dollar bills as a trap for the thief. When the sweat of the body activated the chemicals in the powder the culprit would end up with dirt on the hands that could not be washed away.

It worked! The money disappeared and I went straight to our primary suspect—a loner in the tenth grade who slinked around the halls, walked into open rooms, and made himself a general nuisance. When he answered my knock and opened the door, I said, "Stewart, show me your hands." Bull's-eye! The telltale signs of black splotches covered his palms and fingers. "Come with me," I commanded and then marched him straight to the President's office. Once inside and seated, I recited the facts about the thefts, the powder, and asked the culprit to show his dirty hands. The President, who had more sympathy than I did, spoke in a fatherly tone and addressed him by name, "Stewart, did you steal that money?" A terrified voice quivered, "No Sir, I did not." The President pressed on, restating the incriminating facts and asking again, "Did you steal the money?" Each time, my perp answered, "No Sir, I did not." Finally, the President played the trump card, "Go into the restroom and wash your hands." He obeyed while we waited for the moment of revelation. I had no doubt that we had caught our man—until he walked back into the office and held out his hands. They were perfectly clean! A little soap has washed away the evidence of sin. The President, who had a wry sense of humor, gave me a knowing look and then said to Stewart, "Thanks, son. You can go. Sorry to accuse you."

When the door closed, the President spared me a well-deserved lecture. Instead, he broke into his patented smile and said, "Well, it's back to the drawing board. Let's double check our facts and catch the thief."

Roundly chastised, I went back to work. The powder failed, but the marked bills came to my rescue. The manager of the snack bar called the next day to report the name of the student who had passed a numbered bill. Totally surprised, I immediately called into the office a college freshman and honor student who was the son of a prominent psychiatrist. When confronted with the evidence, he confessed the thefts to me and to the President. Before finalizing disciplinary action, the President instructed me to call the father and tell him the story.

Put yourself in my place. A twenty-four-year-old rookie in the deanship informing a psychiatrist that his son confessed to being a kleptomaniac who couldn't help himself. The father grilled me on every detail, questioned the findings, and implied that I was too young to make judgment on psychological issues. Finally, the father closed the conversation by saying, "Send him home" with a tone of voice that let me know that we had failed his son.

Two lives, two young men. Like so many laughable moments, the scene gets serious when I ask, "What are the consequences?" and "What did I learn?" Their stories do not end there. Stewart, the boy with the clean hands, had to be dismissed when I caught him sneaking a .22 caliber rifle into his dormitory room and showed it off to his roommate. Assuming that the safety was off, he pointed it out the window, took aim at the President's son playing in the yard across the street and pulled the trigger. The bullet ricocheted off the sidewalk and into the back of the President's son, stopping one inch from his spine. My task now included informing each of Stewart's estranged parents of his dismissal, and standing in prayerful vigil over a nine-year-old boy who might be paralyzed for life. The parent's response still haunts me as they cast off responsibility for their son and left me with the thought that I may have been cutting the last lifeline for hope in a young life. In recent years, I have tried to find him again, but even the alumni office gets its mailings returned with the notation, "Bad Address." All I can do is breathe the anxious prayer, "Oh, Lord, find him by your Spirit, surround him with your grace, and guide him into your salvation."

The psychiatrist's son? He enrolled in another college, finished his degree, and rose through corporate ranks to become the highly respected treasurer of his company and a leader in his church.

What did I learn? With the President's gentle reminder, "Check your facts," comes the echo, "Never rush to judgment." Out of a laughable moment when the joke was on me I learned, "Never give up on people until God does." Because he never does, we can't either.

Chapter 5

The Bag That Let the Cat Out

"I've always felt that a big laugh is really a loud noise from the soul saying, 'Ain't it the truth!'"

—Quincy Jones

I HAVE NEVER met a cat I didn't hate. They must feel the same way about me. It isn't just those green eyes that bore right through me. It is acts of vengeance that they wreak on me.

My introduction to the psychology of cats came when I was in graduate school at the University of Michigan. I took a course in criminology from a renowned professor who told us that criminals in prison prefer cats and canaries as their pets. The independent cats defy any attempt to keep them behind bars and singing canaries cannot be caged. I don't know about the canaries, but I sure know about the cats.

"Jackson" was the name of a black tom that we cat-sat when our youngest son lived in a college dormitory that prohibited pets. From the moment that Jackson and I eyed each other open warfare began. Never once did he curl up next to me in a chair or purr when I tried to pet him. When he wasn't ignoring me, he was concocting schemes to bug me. If I were reading the paper, he either squeaked his toys or tried to paw his kitty-litter out of the tray. With the hope of stopping him from climbing on furniture or jumping on counters, I got him a carpet-covered climbing tree. He never touched it. At Christmas time, our conflict peaked. Making sure that he had my attention, he sat under the Christmas tree and batted the gold balls until they fell and broke. When I went to get him, he ran under the tree and hugged the trunk so that I couldn't reach him. If cats can laugh, he guffawed until the day that we gave up and transferred him to our daughter's more cat-compatible household. Our warfare ended in a stalemate.

Zsa-Zsa, a black and white stray, is another story. Sooner or later every little girl picks up a stray cat, brings it home, and pleads with tears to keep it. Debra, our oldest daughter, found the cuddly little creature on the road on the way home from school, gave it the name Zsa-Zsa, and, as a future lawyer, prepared the case to win over her dad. Despite my better judgment, I buckled and Zsa-Zsa became a member of our family with the understanding that Debra had to care for her. All went well until Zsa-Zsa grew big and began to find ways to leave the house late at night. We laughed and said, "She must have a boyfriend out there." That shows you how much we knew about cats and how little attention I paid to her. A couple of mornings later, Zsa-Zsa arrived at our doorstep all bloodied and bruised. At first, we thought that it was an accident, but nighttime excursions and bloodied mornings finally convinced us otherwise. Empirical evidence could not be denied: Zsa-Zsa was a John-John!

A family crisis followed. Our daughter wept to learn that her beloved Zsa-Zsa was a prowling tomcat. In full presidential mode, I took it upon myself the task of telling her that we couldn't keep him, but that I would make sure that Zsa-Zsa/John-John would have a good home at a farm where he could roam at will. So, the next afternoon while Debra was in school, I cancelled my appointments at the office and came home to do the dirty work.

Imagine this setting: Two weeks earlier, I had taken delivery on the new Chevrolet that came with my job as President. As a born and bred Detroiter, I have always taken pride in the automobiles I have driven. This one topped them all. It was a medium blue, four-door sports sedan with soft grey upholstery and all of the chrome trimmings, including wire wheels. My plan was to put Zsa-Zsa/John-John in the car and drive ten miles to a remote farm with the hope that the cat could not find its way back. A neighbor suggested that I put the cat into a burlap bag and stuff it into the trunk of the car until I arrived to my destination, but this sounded like premeditated, first-degree murder to me. At the very least, Zsa-Zsa/John-John deserved an eye-to-eye and face-to-face departure. Besides, I was in a hurry to get the dastardly deed done before Debra arrived home from school. Zsa-Zsa/John-John let me pick him up and put him in the backseat. One look at his battered face where tufts of fur had been chewed out left no doubt about my decision. I climbed into the driver's seat and left town. Less than a mile later, I heard an angry hiss from the back seat and felt claws dig into my back. The revenge of the cat was on. He jumped over my shoulder, dodged the steering wheel, landed on the dashboard, and hit the seat next to me on a route that would take him around and around the inside of car. I was about to stop and catch him when his panic turned into a watery, smelly spray that smeared my new upholstery as well as my shoulder and the dashboard. It was my turn to panic. There was no way that I could drive ten miles in that mess. So, in self-defense, I stopped the car, grabbed the cat, and threw him into the ditch along the roadside. I could only hope that we were far enough away so that he could not find his way home. My last sight of Zsa-Zsa/John-John was a twist of the head to take one look back and then disappear into the underbrush with a flip of the black and white tail.

Today, I might be indicted for cruelty to an innocent animal, but if so, my defense would include the cat's cruelty to a stupid human being. I had to drive home with that mess all over my new car. Cleaning agents failed me and I ended up hosing out the automobile. But, it was never the same. Every time that I got in the driver's seat, I suffered a replay of the episode, complete with the olfactory effects. Far ahead of the regular schedule for trading automobiles, the beautiful blue Chevrolet sports sedan with the wire wheels appeared on the used car lot and I drove away in a new model, having lost a lot of dollars and much more pride.

Zsa-Zsa/John-John never made it home, but he was a survivor. As he disappeared into the underbrush, I can still see the Cheshire Cat grin as he snarled, "Checkmate. I sure fixed your wagon."

So, is there a lesson in the laugh? Totally subdued, I confess, "Zsa-Zsa/John-John is proof that college presidents with PhDs do not know everything."

Chapter 6

The Tennis Racket That Unstrung a President

"With mirth and laughter let old wrinkles come."

—William Shakespeare

EVERYONE WITH A computer has seen the circulating story about the graduating class at the University of Maryland. To assure a thoroughly secular commencement, university authorities ruled that there could be no prayer, religious song, or even mention of the name of God. When the class president got up to give his speech, all of the graduates pinched their noses and sneezed, "AH CHOO!" With a feigned look of innocence, the class president answered, "God bless you." Rolling laughter gave way to thunderous applause.

New college presidents soon learn that executive authority is no match for student creativity. Way back in 1947, when I enrolled as a freshman at Spring Arbor Junior College, students felt the heavy hand of in loco parentis along with denominational discipline in the regulations governing campus life. One of those rules involved co-eds who dared not go without nylon hose, even while wearing bobby sox and saddle shoes. The first glimpse of Janet Voorheis, my future wife, showed me a creative violator of the rules. Looking up from my position as quarterback on the freshman flag football team, she was a vision of beauty walking along the sidelines, complete in a cheerleader's sweater, skirt, bobby socks, saddle shoes, and the line of nylon hose up the back of her legs. "Ah ha," I thought, "I am going to meet that woman and ask her for a date." My running back, however, saw me look and said, "She is the college pastor's daughter, wearing fake hose and a touch of lipstick." Sure enough, I learned that co-eds who rebelled against the regulation for wearing hose worked together to paint a line up the back of their legs and defied the Dean of Men to enforce the rule by closer observation or inspection. I reacted by writing her off as a "Preacher's Brat" and a rebellious "Townie" who dared to challenge the rules of the "Gown." How wrong I was. Six months later, I asked her out and three years later, I married her.

Don't place all of the blame upon conservative religious schools. In the first summer of my presidency at Spring Arbor College, I attended a campus-planning workshop at Harvard. One of the sessions included a tour of student housing designed to accommodate both sexes in the same hall. Our guide told us that Harvard solved the concern of parents about co-ed housing by requiring that the door to the room remain open when one sex visited another. Our laughter could hardly be contained when we walked past a room with book of matches keeping the door open. Creative students not only met the letter of the law but used the match book as a warning not to disturb whatever was going on behind the "open" door.

Fundamentalist schools get the biggest laughs because of the disjuncture between their rules and reality. Bob Jones University, for instance, boycotted Billy Graham from speaking on campus because he consorted with liberal Christians in his crusades. Students of the university quickly saw humor in the ridiculous and sent out word, "Bob Jones University is so opposed to Billy Graham that it will not even let 'Graham crackers' be served in the dining hall."

Liberty University, founded by Jerry Falwell, had behavioral regulations as strict as its fundamentalist theology. Students who could not keep up with all of the rules found the solution by using their own theology to beat the code. Liberty University soon became known as the place where, "It is easier to ask forgiveness than to get permission."

For me, the prize of all prizes belongs to the students at Greenville College back in the late 1960s. My good friend Glenn Richardson had just been elected as President of the college after achieving considerable success in the field of business. Early in his administration, he invited me to campus to speak at their annual Minister's Conference. In our first meeting, he confided that the change of worlds from the profit-making corporation to the academic community baffled him. Even though he was twenty years my senior, he sought my counsel.

"How do you sleep at night?" he asked.

I admitted that occasionally I had fitful nights, but that I was blessed with the gift of sleep and the bonus of naps.

As if he didn't hear me, Glenn went on, "When I go to bed at night, I have a pad and pencil on my nightstand. When I get up in the morning, the pad is full."

Red flags were flying. I knew that President Richardson's tenure would be short unless he learned to leave the job at the office. Wisely or not, I recommended, "For heaven's sake, throw away the pad and go to sleep."

The next morning, I saw why student creativity is more than a match for executive authority. Ministers from several states arrived on campus for their annual conference and lined up to register in the administration building just outside the President's office. At that time Greenville College had a hard and fast rule that students could not wear shorts on campus unless they were going to a physical education class or an athletic practice. While I was standing in the lobby visiting with the incoming ministers, the huge entrance door opened and in walked a shapely blonde co-ed, all in white, wearing the tightest of sweaters and the shortest of shorts. Smiling demurely, she cooed, "Excuse me," and walked triumphantly through the line of ministers that had parted like the Red Sea for the children of Israel. Pastoral eyes popped at the sight, pious talk came to a halt, and holy heads turned away. No one doubted that she had been set up by other students to flaunt the rule in full view of the ministerial visitors. But, what could they say? Under her arm she carried a tennis racket!

What started out as a Minister's Conference turned into a minister's protest. Before the day was out, a group of ministerial leaders had notified the President that they wanted to "wait" on him and deal with the issue. We can laugh at the episode now, but at the time it was dead serious. I am sure that the President's pad filled up that night because, after a few more months in office, he resigned and returned to his field of excellence—the more manageable world of business.

Survivors in the college presidency live by this rule: *In a contest between presidential authority and student creativity, students win every time.* The same applies to parents, pastors, and professors, or any elder in authority who is challenged by the younger generation. To survive, we need to flex, laugh, and move on.

Chapter 7

The Chapel with the Cha-Cha-Cha

> "Deep, shared, and mutual laughter
> is the stuff of friendship."
>
> —Richard Beck

COLLEGE PRESIDENTS ARE not known for joshing one another. You might read about friendly bets between presidential archrivals on the outcome of a football game, such as sending apples from Washington versus oranges from Florida, but that is about the extent of it. On rare occasions, however, a college president cannot resist the temptation to poke fun at a colleague.

In my first presidency at Spring Arbor College I invited Dorr Demaray, President of Seattle Pacific College to give a chapel address. The two schools were sister institutions in affiliation with the Free Methodist Church of North America. Seattle Pacific, however, had the reputation of being the most liberal in student standards while Spring Arbor held the opposite reputation. Dr. Demaray enjoyed the distinction as dean among the presidents of our denominational schools. A godly spirit, a gentle soul, and a winning speaker added special grace to his leadership.

On the way to the morning chapel, I took President Demaray past the construction site for our new student commons at Spring Arbor College. It was the sign of my success. Huge piles of dirt bordered the hole in the ground where the foundations were being laid. From someplace in my travels, I had borrowed the caption for the construction sign that also announced the building of the Stanley and Dorothy Kresge Student Center. With deference to the students and local community, the sign read, "EXCUSE OUR DUST, DEVELOP WE MUST." As we approached the site, my pride went cold. In the middle of the night some students had taken a can of paint and brushed a bright red change in the "D" of the word "DUST." The sign now read, "EXCUSE OUR BUST, DEVELOP WE MUST." President Demaray burst into hilarious laughter. As best I could, I also laughed. Because of my past history for pulling pranks, I thought that the re-painted sign showed a stroke of genius, but inwardly I had to deal with wounded pride.

In the chapel service, Dr. Demaray did not let up. In his introduction, he commended the college and its president for our commitment to the Spring Arbor Concept and the "serious study of the Christian liberal arts." Then, with a twinkle in his eye for which he was known, he wondered aloud how this fit with the sign that read, "EXCUSE OUR

BUST, DEVELOP WE MUST." Alumni, at reunions, still talk about the moment.

Unbeknownst to me, President Demaray also visited Spring Arbor College to scout out the young president who might be a candidate for his position because he planned to retire in two years. The construction sign may have helped my future candidacy because I soon received a return invitation to speak in the chapel at Seattle Pacific College. Awed by my first visit to Seattle and Seattle Pacific College, I took my chapel address very seriously. In contrast with the daily chapel of fifty minutes at Spring Arbor, SPC held three services a week of thirty minutes in length. Knowing this, I planned for a highly disciplined and academically sophisticated twenty-minute address. I had a lesson to learn. After the students were seated, the Dean of the Chapel turned numerous announcements about campus events into a standup comedy. Almost ten minutes passed and he still had them laughing. For the finale, he admitted, "I don't know what's coming next?" Out from the wings danced a mini-skirted cheerleading squad doing high-kicks with the precision of the Rockettes. Once on the stage they picked sombreros off the floor and did a lusty Mexican hat dance complete with the raucous rejoinder of "Cha-Cha-Cha" from the chapel congregation. I could only think back to our recent controversy at Spring Arbor College when conservative constituents questioned how high the cheerleaders could kick once school policy was changed to permit them to wear skirts rather slacks with their outfits.

One look at my watch and I knew that my twenty-minute speech was doomed. With fourteen minutes left in the chapel, President Demaray got up to introduce me, and sure enough, he retold the story of the construction sign at Spring Arbor

College. Changing my planned response to his introduction, I countered by saying that I had never been in a chapel where the anthem was the Mexican Hat Dance complete with the congregation chanting "Cha-Cha-Cha" rather than "Amen." Quick to catch on, the students saw the give-and-take between presidents and added their roar to the laughter. I then winged a nine-minute recap of my speech and finished on time. I do not remember my subject or what I said, but forty years later, Ray Bakke, one of the students in the chapel and now a leading urban missiologist, surprised me by reciting every point I made.

I must have done something right because the next year President Demaray announced his retirement and the Seattle Pacific College Board elected me as his successor. To this day, he is my proof that college presidents can be holy and have a sense of humor. If we learn to laugh at ourselves, God will laugh with us as he saves us from ourselves.

Chapter 8

The Untimely Twist of a Tangled Tongue

"While it is perfectly human to degrade our enemies,
it's divine to see the humor in yourself."

—Anonymous

PRESIDENTIAL INAUGURATIONS ARE like tribal rituals for the academic community and rites of passage for incoming leaders. "Pomp and Circumstance" is played at its peak when scholars in multi-colored gowns, hoods, and caps march in solemn procession down the aisle. Choirs sing, orchestras play, solemn charges are given, presidential medals are conferred, a visiting dignitary speaks, and the new leader casts a vision of hope for the future.

A key to the academic stature of the college or university at a presidential inauguration is the celebrity status of the guest speaker. Everyone starts out with an invitation to the President of the United States followed by Billy Graham and works downward from there. Institutions with strong ambitions will score a coup if they can bring in a speaker of national or international stature with instant name recognition. No expense is spared for a presidential inauguration because it is the moment when a college or university puts its best foot forward to establish its brand of academic quality. The assumption is that it is a once-in-a-generation event even though the average tenure of presidents is less than five years.

Three presidential inaugurations mark my leadership for three institutions of higher education over a period of thirty-three years. Each one had a special purpose related to the future of the school. Working backward from my last presidency at Asbury Theological Seminary: our inaugural goals in 1983 were to position Asbury as a theological leader in the evangelical Christian community and as the flagship for seminaries in the Wesleyan tradition across the world. To accomplish our first goal, we invited Charles Colson—notorious for his role in the Watergate scandal, but later anointed for his Christian prison ministry—to keynote the inauguration. To advance our second goal, we obtained a grant to telecast by satellite the inaugural events to our alumni and friends on downlinks across North America.

The presidential inauguration at Seattle Pacific College in 1969 had its own symbolic value. Because of a financial crisis we delayed the inauguration for a year until we had the situation under control and then rented the Seattle Opera House with all of its sophisticated reputation to send the message—especially to the worlds of Seattle and the Northwest—that all was well with the soul of our institution. I shall never forget the grandeur that greeted us when the academic procession entered the hall. A full house with orchestra and choir led us on the march to the rostrum where our senator, mayor, and business leaders welcomed Arthur S. Flemming, President of three colleges—Ohio Wesleyan, University of Oregon, and Macalister College—as well as Secretary of Health, Education, and Welfare in the Eisenhower administration, as our distinguished speaker. Prior to the ceremony itself, we had an Inaugural Collegium on campus led by Ernest Boyer, soon to be appointed as U.S. Commissioner on Education for the United States. Our motive was obvious. In the mind of the media, Seattle Pacific College had the dubious image of the "Little Sunday School by the Canal" under the shadow of the University of Washington. We were out to change that image and gain academic recognition as a Christian college of significance in American higher education.

Much more was at stake in my first presidential inauguration at Spring Arbor College in 1963. After leaving the faculty at Ohio State University and asking to be released from my contract at the University of Michigan, I accepted the presidency of Spring Arbor Junior College in 1961 with the assignment to build a four-year, fully accredited, Christian liberal arts college. Again, we delayed the inaugural date for a year until we could discontinue the high school academy and lay the groundwork for the four-year program. Everything was on paper and the risks were high—so high, in fact, that the inauguration took on the seriousness of a life-and-death issue. Pushing every button, we worked to bring the power of the Republican Party to our campus. Dan Karn (Chair of Consumer's Power Company and "Mr. Republican" in Michigan) and Tyronne Gillespie (Counsel for Dow Chemical) combined their clout and convinced Governor George Romney to accept our invitation to give the inaugural address. To make sure that we matched sophistication with their clout, I asked Charles Williams, Vice-President for Development, to preside over the event. Charles enjoyed the reputation as one of the most eloquent of platform speakers. His brilliance of thought, depth of feeling, and smoothness of delivery would certainly impress our special guests and raise our identity with the academic delegates.

Charles and Vicki, his wife, had a funny side to go with their sophistication. At home and in the company of friends they loved to twist words or put the "em-PHA-sis" on the wrong "syl-LAB-ull." Hotel Hayes in Jackson, for instance, became the "Hose Haytel", a tangled tongue became a "tonguled tang," and a garbled newspaper article reported "a defective on the police farce" who arrested a man for being "under the alca-fluence of inka-hol." They never stopped laughing at the college president who always talked about faculty members as "aca-MAGICIANS," and never missed the opportunity to turn a pun, such as the one about the dermatologist who started his practice "from a scratch" or the archeologist who "found his fortune in ruins." The best laugh, however, came when Charles told about taking Vicki away from her home in Kansas and bringing her to Michigan. "Whenever she gets homesick," he said, "I just beat the dust out of the davenport."

All these jokes were put aside at my inauguration. After a dignified march down the aisle and up the stairs with the platform party, flags were placed, marshals were seated, and the music stopped. Charles stepped to the podium, gestured for the audience to be seated, and with full platform voice announced, "Welcome to this HYSTERICAL occasion." The solemn scene went dead silent and by the time that Charles corrected himself he could not control the little waves of awkward laughter moving through the crowd. He had been caught in his own tongue-twisting humor. I tried to laugh as well, but only through the depth of my disappointment. After all of our anxious preparation to present Spring Arbor College as a refined academic institution, I felt as if we had been reduced to a laughing stock. While I stewed inside, Governor Romney roared with understanding laughter. When he got up to speak, he likened little Spring Arbor College to the compact auto for which he had become famous as the CEO who turned around American Motors. "Yes," he said, "both the car and the college are small, but made at the highest quality in response to a special need." George Romney saved the day and taught me to lighten up. Like the best-laid plans of mice and men, our perfectionistic programming can always go awry, and when the laugh is on you, it is a powerful antidote for exaggerated expectations.

Chapter 9

The Wet Finger on Ancient Crystal

"Laughter is the shortest distance between two people."

—Victor Borge

A COLLEGE PRESIDENT is supposed to be the genial host and gracious guest at all of the dinners, receptions, and parties that go with the job. This means looking wise, speaking smart, and inserting little gems of delicate humor into the conversation of the evening. Some college presidents have natural gifts for this role. Others have to work at it and learn by failure. Count me in the latter group.

You have already met C. Dorr Demaray, my predecessor at Seattle Pacific College, as my model of a gracious spirit and genial host in the presidency. Before I was elected to that position, he and his wife, Grace, invited me to be their guest for dinner in Hillford House, the President's home. Awe took over as I stepped in the dining room and saw the exquisite table for which the First Lady was known. While waiting for dinner, Dorr showed me his crystal collection. Glasses, tumblers, and goblets filled the wall of the dining room, row upon row, shelf upon shelf. President Demaray was a collector of antique crystal glassware.

I came to rapt attention as Dorr showed me the prizes of his collection. As a young president, I envied him and his enthusiasm as he picked up glass after glass and spoke its history. Right then and there, I decided that I, too, had to take a hobby that would make me an expert in some field of fascination. One by one, Dorr took glassware from the shelves, named the piece by vintage, and then pinged it with his finger so that I could hear the ring. Out of that sound came a story. With historical precision Dorr recited the date of the piece and the details of its making. Then, to prove the quality of the glass, he wet his finger and ran it around the edge until the crystal sang. Even I could hear the difference in the purity of the sound from one glass to another. My host went on to explain how the lead content affected the tone and determined the quality of the crystal.

Memory of that moment stayed with me after I was elected as successor to President Demaray. I had no antique collections of my own, but I used the story to talk about this special revelation of a man who thoroughly enjoyed every moment of life and never stopped finding excitement in such little things as the quality of the ring in the crystal.

Soon after my election as President, I had a chance to use the story at a private dinner hosted for Jan and me by the Chair of the Music Department, Wayne Balch, and his wife,

Dorothy (or "Do" as she is affectionately called). The Balches went all out to set an exquisite table with the finest of china and crystal to complement delectable food. After dessert had been served and we settled back to enjoy a final cup of coffee, I commented on the fine cut and sparkle of the crystal water glasses at our place. Then, taking one up in my hands, I began, "Do you know how to show the quality of crystal in this glass? I learned the secret from Dr. Demaray." Curious heads shook "No" as I lifted the glass and pinged the side three or four times with the tip of my fingernail. A clear ring led me to say, "Ah, ha. This is a good piece. If the glass had a lot of lead in it, the ring would have been dull." Even the Chair of the Music Department seemed satisfied with my tonal ear. So, I charged on, saying, "But here is the real way to test the quality of the crystal." Wetting my finger with my tongue, I deftly touched the rim of the glass and ran my finger around the edge. Luck was with me because the crystal started to sing immediately. Moving my finger faster and faster on the rim, a pure tone reached a pitch that almost hurt the ears. Glancing up and hoping for applause, my eyes met the eyes of our hostess, Do. Her jaw had dropped, her mouth was open, and her eyes had the fright of a fawn caught in the headlights. She blurted out, "THAT is my mother's heirloom crystal!" The panic shifted from her eyes to mine as I realized what I had done. Do feared that the shrill and penetrating pitch would shatter the glass. We just looked at each other until Do heaved a sigh of relief and began to laugh. She had me and she knew it.

More than forty years have gone by since the night of our dinner. Whenever we meet, Do Balch always begins with the greeting, "Mr. President." But, before I can answer, she adds, "Remember the crystal?" The laugh is still on me. At the same time that Do honors me as her President, she never lets me forget how human I am. Thank God for colleagues who speak the truth with love as "unpaid guardians of our soul."

Chapter 10

The Buried Head on a Tilted Table

> "Humor is merely tragedy standing on its head with its pants torn."
>
> —Irvin S. Cobb

ANY COLLEGE OR university president who claims to have no interest in his or her public image is a liar. More than ego is involved. Fred Smith, my mentor, made no bones about it when he told me, "You are the face of the institution." There are times, however, when you'd prefer that your face didn't show.

When I accepted the presidency of Seattle Pacific College in 1968, our agreement with the Board of Trustees included an annual physical examination. Even though I was only thirty-nine years old, our trustees understood the stress of the job and the need for a president who was physically fit. I didn't realize what I was in for. When I registered at the well-known Virginia Mason Clinic with Dr. Randolph Pillow as my primary physician, I encountered a battery of tests that went from head to toe and turned me inside out. When Dr. Pillow ordered the barium-air contrast test to check my gastrointestinal track, I blissfully made my way to the clinic for a quick stop between appointments in the President's office. How wrong I was! Not only did the test consume far more time that I expected and hurt as much as any pain I had ever experienced, but the aftereffects bordered on disaster. The first time I had the test, Jan and I were scheduled to fly to Europe the next day and we still had shopping to do before we left. Immediately after the exam, we planned to drive to the University District where I did my shopping at a men's store. I was also scheduled to meet a candidate for the Dean's position at SeaTac Airport and host a luncheon with our faculty search committee.

Those of you who have had barium-air contrast examinations will be far ahead of me. After having your guts blown up like a balloon, you are then given a large bottle of barium, best described as watery chalk, to drink down in gulps. When the test is over, the nurse invites you to evacuate the barium from your system before getting dressed and being dismissed. Because I was in a hurry to go shopping, I obeyed as best I could and left early. All went well until I dropped Jan off in front of the men's shop and began looking for a parking place. I found one about three blocks from the store, parked, and got out to walk the short distance to meet her. Half way there I was hit by a sensation that turned into life's most embarrassing moment. I lost total control as the rest of the barium, to use the nurse's word, "evacuated." I left the sidewalk, went into a parking lot, and stood cross-legged against the fender of someone's car. Total paralysis! My car was parked a block south, Jan was waiting two blocks north, and I could not move. Sheer agony showed on my face, so much so that a man coming into the parking lot stopped to ask if something was wrong. I could only hope that he didn't recognize the face of the President of Seattle Pacific College. Painfully, I answered. "Yes," and told him my dilemma. His sympathy prompted me to ask, "Would you be willing to take my car keys and go around the block to get my car?" To this day, I cannot believe that I gave a total stranger the keys to my beloved Ford Mustang car with the hope that he would come back.

After agonizing minutes, the welcome sight of the Mustang came into view. I took out my billfold and offered the man a ten-dollar bill for his trouble, but he said, "No, I know what you are going through. I've been through it myself." So, off I went to pick up Jan and head for home, thoroughly chagrined and totally humanized. But, when I described to her the scene of me standing in the parking lot, the picture turned to comedy. Jan and I could not stop laughing, and to this day, we know why good humor is made from the ludicrous. Imagine a young college president, a well-known face in the community, standing cross-legged in a parking lot, completely out of control, and totally embarrassed. Only God's good grace spared me from a passerby who might have seen me, smiled, and gushed, "Why hello, Dr. McKenna, how are you doing?"

When I returned to Dr. Pillow's office for the report, my first question was, "Dr. have you ever had a barium-air contrast exam?" A devilish little smile crossed his face as he answered, "No." Still feeling the aftereffects of the episode, I mounted my soapbox and told him, "I do not believe that a doctor should ever order any examination for a patient that he has not taken himself!" He just smiled and ordered the next test.

On the same go-around of tests that went through my whole gastrointestinal system, Dr. Pillow ordered a sigmoidoscopy that he himself would perform. This is an examination for polyps in the lowest portion of the intestinal track. The procedure requires the patient to bare the rear and bend over an examining table that is tilted so that the head is down and the rump is up. Once again, a proud, young college president found himself in a compromised position where titles and degrees do not count. No sooner had I readied myself for the examination when the door opened and by peripheral vision, I could see the white shoes of a group of nurses. Then, I heard a voice announce to my doctor, "This is the new class of nurses from Seattle Pacific College."

How far can a college president bury his tell-tale curly head into the bottom of a tilted examining table? I nosed down and burrowed deeply into the leather, hoping against hope that no one would recognize my face. I knew that Dr. Pillow would never betray me, but I wasn't sure that a student nurse wouldn't gasp and speak my name. Instead, I suspect that my doctor shooed them away with a "Get Lost" look. When I dared look up, he simply said, "Sorry," and proceeded with the probe.

If you think that you are reading a fairy tale, "You ain't heard nothin' yet." By now you have surmised that I have a problem in my gastrointestinal track. You are right. Thirty years after the incident in Dr. Pillow's, we returned to Seattle and to annual examinations. Our new primary physician read my history and recommended a colonoscopy to make sure that the track was clear. After drinking a gallon of colyte that competed with the torture of water-boarding, I went through the miseries of preparing for the procedure. The next morning, I found myself lying flat on my back with an old friend, the examining table, wearing a hospital gown with southern exposure, and curled into a fetal position awaiting the arrival of the doctor. The door opened. In walked a pert and pretty young nurse with her eyes glued to the chart in her hand. Absentmindedly, she spoke her name and then, with furrowed brow, she looked up to ask, "Are you THE David McKenna?" "Oh no," I thought, "Here we go again." Sure enough, after I confessed who I was, she chirped, "I'm a graduate of SPU and I'll be your attending nurse."

Three presidencies, five earned degrees, and ten honorary doctorates lost all of their potency in that moment. I lay there like a chunk of flesh with no place to hide my head. Natural instinct saved the day when I regained my composure enough to mutter, "When did you graduate?" Awkward moments followed until we found common ground in the latest books that we were reading. Some place in the middle of this stumbling conversation the doctor came in, sodium pentathol took over, and I drifted into the mercy of a dream world.

Every book on leadership makes humility as a virtue of greatness. If so, I recommend that programs in leadership development include at least one of the these procedures, a barium-air contrast examination, a sigmoidoscopy, or a colonoscopy. Any one of them is a sure cure for the pride that goes along with the presidency, especially if someone recognizes your face.

Chapter 11

The Blind Sledder on an Alpine Run

"Laughter is the closest thing to the grace of God."

—Karl Barth

SEATTLE, LIKE ROME, was built on seven hills. At least, it was until Denny Hill got sluiced across Elliott Bay to level the land for the building of the Space Needle as the centerpiece for the Seattle World's Fair in 1962. Queen Anne Hill is one of the six hills that remain. It has special significance for me because the campus of Seattle Pacific University occupies a choice spot on the northern slope that begins high on the hill and reaches down to the Washington Ship Canal. Hillford House, the President's home, sits on the steep incline of Sixth Avenue overlooking the President's office two blocks below. We often said that the hill served as the training ground for climbing

Mt. Rainier. Trudging upward, our students had to press against the hill. The downward walk was equally challenging. Students had to lean back and walk gingerly with their heels as brakes.

Put a rare Seattle snowstorm into the picture. When it snows in Seattle, everything stops. The city is not prepared for icy streets and its unskilled citizens get stuck trying to get up sloping driveways. The Sixth Avenue hill slicing through the Seattle Pacific University campus is particularly formidable. Neither cars nor walkers dare to go up or down. Students, however, are undaunted. Once the snow comes and the university is shut down, celebration begins. Borrowing food trays from the dining commons as makeshift sleds, they set up races down the hill. Most often, the food trays become whirling dervishes that spin out of control, crash into the curb, and leave their riders buried in a snow bank, but squealing with laughter and eager to try again. Day and night, the party goes on.

After two days of being snowbound in the President's home, my Type A personality got the best of me and I decided that I would try to walk down the hill to the President's office. Dressed in a business suit, white shirt, rep tie, tasseled loafers, London Fog trench coat, and carrying my brief case, I stepped out the door and into the company of at least fifty students waiting their turn to slide down the hill. Peering down the icy street where students in boots and cleats slid backwards trying to get up to the top, I knew that I could never make it wearing leather-soled loafers.

Hoots and hollers greeted me. With one voice, the students raised the challenge and handed me a food tray. "No way," I said, "That's downright dangerous. I'm used to sliding with a sled." At that moment, I made my fatal mistake of telling them about my exploits on a sled as a youngster growing up in Michigan where we had ice and snow from November to March or April. "If I had a sled," I bragged, "I would give it a try."

Out of nowhere, a hooded figure appeared over the top of the hill dragging a full-sized Silver Flyer sled behind him. He was King of the Hill because he took passengers on his back, double-deck fashion, one lying on top of the other. I recognized him as Kermit Helsel, the son of a faculty member who lived nearby and evidently had the sled stored in the garage. "Here it is," my challengers yelled, "Kermit will give you a ride to your office."

My credibility with the students hung in the balance.

"Look at me, " I pleaded, "I'm in a business suit with a long coat and a briefcase."

They wouldn't let up.

"Just lie down on his back and use one hand to hold your briefcase."

Like a condemned man going to his death, I lay down on Kermit's back, grabbed hold of the sled with one hand and crooked the other over my shoulder to carry the briefcase. As far as I know, no one took pictures, but if they had, it would have won the prize for comedy. The president of a university in full business dress lay prone on the back of a student in boots and a woodsman's jacket complete with hood.

Ear-shattering cheers went along with the extra-healthy push that I felt at the back of sled. Once over the brow of the hill, we picked up speed on the snowy slope that had turned to ice. I hung on with a one-handed death grip as we plummeted through the first block and toward the second where my office was located. I realized that my life was in the hands of a faculty member's son and wondered if he might want revenge for my executive decisions on faculty matters, especially on benefits for their families. Closing my eyes, I just gripped tight and hoped for the best.

When I took a chance and re-opened my eyes, I saw that we could not stop at the entrance to the administration building, but were heading pell-mell toward a dead end where Sixth Avenue intersected with Bertona Street, an equally steep hill leading to the bottom of Queen Anne Hill. Looking down at my driver, I couldn't believe what I saw. His head was turned at a right angle. With the dead end looming ahead, he was looking the other way. I shut my eyes again, expecting the worst. But no, with slick precision, I felt the back of the sled skid to the left and the front go right as we made the turn and continued down the final leg at breakneck speed.

Opening my eyes, I saw the head of my driver now cocked 90 degrees to the left as the sled plummeted straight ahead. Danger again loomed in front of us. We were just a block from the ground-level street where traffic inched along through the snow. Under my body I felt the feet of my driver reach out to brake the sled and make a spinning turn into a campus parking lot. Another cluster of students cheered with "thumbs up" and hands reached out to help me rise without rolling off the sled. Standing on wobbly feet, I had only one question, "Kermit, what were you doing looking sideways? We could have been killed." The students already knew the answer. They clapped and howled as Kermit explained, "Looking straight ahead, I am blind in both eyes. But I do have some peripheral vision. The only way that I can see where I am going is to turn my head from side to side."

I needed more than a minute to regain my sense of humor. After all, I had risked my life on a speeding sled with a blind man as my driver. When the students saw the shock on my face, they went out of their way to assure me that they too had ridden down the hill with Kermit and no one had ever crashed. Then, we started a laugh that is heard every time I meet students who were on the hill that night. They never fail to remind me that I had set myself up by bragging about my exploits on a sled when I was a boy in Michigan. But, they always remember the comic sight of me on Kermit's back and the look on my face when he told me that he could only see straight when he was looking sideways. The laugh was on me and I learned never to start a conversation with the younger generation by saying, "When I was your age . . ." If they don't write you off, they will make you prove it.

Chapter 12

The Jokester Who Should Have Succeeded Nixon

"Christian faith is the most humorous point of view that a person can take."

—Kierkegaard

MY FIFTEEN MINUTES of fame began with a laugh on me. The culprit set me up and worked his scheme to perfection.

Our President's home on the campus of Seattle Pacific University stood in the crosshairs of men's and women's residence halls, above and below. We loved being in the center of action, except when a 1500 amp stereo boomed out of the William Tell Overture. Or, when the outdoor faucets on the home served as fill-up stations for the annual balloon fight between Ashton men and Hill women. Our front porch was also the final stop in the initiation rite for newly-engaged Ashton men. After being stripped to their briefs, the ritual began with a ceremonial toss into the ice-cold Washington Ship Canal. Fished out on a long pole, the entourage paraded its blindfolded victim up the hill to the porch of the President's home where they rang the doorbell and ran. They knew that Jan, First Lady of the campus, never turned anyone away. She answered the door, then ran for a large towel and a warm blanket before fixing some special snack to make the perpetrators jealous.

The jokester who started the clock on my fifteen minutes of fame knew all about our vulnerable position in the middle of the dorms. It happened on November 21, 1979, the day after Ronald Reagan was elected President. At precisely six o'clock in the morning loud rings on the bedside phone turned me over to grope for the instrument and mumble a sleepy, "Hello."

"Mr. President," a no-nonsense voice boomed, "there is a pantry raid going on in the women's dorm *right now*!" I sat up, startled wide awake. "Who is this?" The response back in the roar of laughter that says, "I *gotcha!*" I was in no mood for fun until the laughing voice confessed, "This is Mark Hatfield." Whatever rage I felt gave way to deference for the man whom I considered my model for Christian leadership.

"Sorry to give you such a rude awakening," Senator Hatfield apologized, "but it is nine o'clock in Washington and I wanted to get to you right away. Will you let me nominate you as Secretary of Education for President Reagan?" I went numb. Secretary of Education meant being the number-one educator in the nation and a participating member in the most powerful team in the world. No fantasy of mine had ever embraced such a possibility. Almost immediately, I said, "Yes," along with the question, "What should I do?" Senator Hatfield stopped me short: "Do nothing. I'll nominate you today and, if God is in it, it will be." On that note of mutual submission to the will of God, we agreed to stay in touch while we waited.

A month or more went by without any word. The media floated trial balloons about potential candidates with an emphasis upon diversity in the last position to balance out the President's Cabinet. Early in January, my impatience took hold and I called Senator Hatfield with a plan for getting support from high-ranking friends in education, religion, and government. He chided me for my Wesleyan activism and invoked again his Calvinist leanings, "If God is in it, it will be." Then, the unexpected happened. After a speech on education at a Seattle luncheon, word circulated downtown to the head of the Reagan campaign for the Northwest. Jim Munn asked me to meet with him and spin out my philosophy, policy, and practices of education. Within hours after our meeting he rode a red-eye flight to Washington with the word for Vice-President-Elect George H. W. Bush, "I've found your man for Education." Word leaked to the media and, the next day, I found myself answering calls from Eastern newspapers and holding a press conference on campus for television outlets. As best we know, my name went forward as one of two finalists at an all night meeting of the selection committee at the Army-Navy Club in D.C. From here on, second hand reports informed us that on President-Elect Reagan's return flight from a meeting with the President of Mexico was interrupted by a phone call from a prominent corporate executive and the largest personal contributor to the Reagan campaign. A devout Mormon, the individual reputedly exerted his clout by saying, "We didn't get our man in Commence or Labor. We want our man in Education." With that, the name of Terrel H. Bell, Commissioner for Higher Education in Utah, became the new and preferred candidate for the position.

When we awakened the next morning, television carried the picture of Terrell Bell leaving a limousine and walking into Blair House for his appointment. What had started out as a friendly laugh turned into a cruel joke when the cameras panned across the brass plate on the back of the chairs in the Cabinet room and showed the name, "Terrel H. Bell." Like baby bear coming home, I found myself grumbling, "Someone's sitting in my chair."

Thirty years later, I still have to work through the issues to regain my perspective. Intellectually, I accept Senator Hatfield's wisdom and admit that God was not in it. Confirmation comes when I remember that politics, not competence, ruled the appointments of undersecretaries and the Secretary himself had to have his speeches written or screened for political correctness. God knew that I would soon be in trouble. Emotionally, however, the spirit of adventure still makes me wonder about "the road not travelled." My wife, Jan, and I had worked through our fears about a cross-country move into the morass of Foggy Bottom. We were ready to go, but not without the caveat, "Lord, if it means losing my faith, my marriage, or my family, don't let me go." When I remember this prayer, I admit again, "God knows best."

At the time, however, God and I had a spat. I felt as if he had set me up to let me down. Not without anger, I asked, "Why?" While nursing my wounds over the loss of the position, I traveled to Washington to counsel with Senator Hatfield. He listened patiently to my self-pity, mixed emotions, and lingering regrets. After I finished, the Senator said that he knew how I felt because he had gone through a similar experience.

In 1968, on the night when Richard Nixon received the Republican nomination for President, the nation awaited the obvious news that Mark Hatfield would be named as his vice-presidential choice. Reporters crammed the halls of Hatfield's hotel, hoping to be the first to break the news. Mark and Antoinette Hatfield waited until midnight. No news came. With a prayer of commitment, they went to bed, still expecting the call to come sometime in the middle of the night. But, when they awakened in the morning and turned on the news, Nixon had named Spiro Agnew as his vice-presidential choice.

My little snit with God seemed so small. Shame took over as I heard the Senator's story. Here I was, complaining about the loss of the last and lowest position on Ronald Reagan's Cabinet when Mark Hatfield spoke with peace about being betrayed for the position that was only a breath from the presidency. A flood of regret washed over me when I realized that I was in the presence of the man who might have changed the course of our national history. To this day, when I replay Senator Hatfield's fun-filled words—"Mr. President, I want to report a panty raid in the women's dorm"—I also hear a man of God saying, "If God is in it, it will be." I can only regret that he did not get the chance to bring his faith, his integrity, and his humor to occupy the White House.

Chapter 13

The Short Arm of the Law

"Against the shout of laughter, nothing can stand."

—Mark Twain

COLLEGE TRADITIONS THAT smack of student humor usually bypass the president. Oftentimes, these traditions lack the dignity expected of the president's office or may even be an embarrassment to the institution.

In 1970, I attended a Harvard football game as the guest of Chuck White, a family friend and student at the university. I remember the football game as an upgraded high school contest, but at halftime I was introduced to one of the most memorable of Harvard traditions. When the bedraggled Harvard band took the field everything became fair game. They parodied the reputation of the university, made fun of its alumni, and skewered politicians at the national level. While everyone else roared with laughter, I found myself identifying with President Nathan Pusey, sitting somewhere in the stands. I knew that he was thinking, "How will I smooth the ruffled feathers of our wealthy alumni?"

Wheaton College (Illinois) has a tradition that is equally hazardous to the president. In the final chapel service of the year at which the president speaks, tradition calls for some kind of ingenious student prank. President Hudson Armerding, a dear friend and former Navy Commander, took every precaution to avoid the obvious but more often than not the students won. Alumni of that era still talk about the final chapel when President Armerding stood to speak and every student eye went up to the ceiling. Sliding down invisible wires were mice. When they reached the middle of the chapel, directly over the heads of the student body, they were dropped, little parachutes opened, and they floated down to shrieking co-eds and snickering men. Knowing Hudson as well as I do, I am sure that he gave a short lecture from the helm and then very effectively delivered his final chapel talk.

Herfy's Run at Seattle Pacific University is also an institution. Ashton Residence Hall is directly across the street from the Hilliard House, the President's home. Someplace back in the late 1960s or early 1970s, the men of fourth-floor Ashton started a rite of spring called "The Herfy's Run." Lining up their cars in a caravan, they circled the campus, blowing their horns, and then honked their way through the surrounding neighborhood on Queen Anne Hill before dipping down to the Interbay road between Queen Anne and Magnolia Hills on the way to Herfy's fast food hamburgers. By pre-arrangement, they took over the restaurant, ordered their hamburgers and shakes, and then recapped the year by giving little speeches about the exploits of their members.

Somewhere along the line, an enterprising fourth-floor resident proposed an invitation to the President to join their Herfy's Run. When I agreed to go, their plans became more elaborate. Decorations were added to the cars in my honor. When they picked me up, I walked to the lead car under the arched arms of students as they chanted my name. To make the event extra special, they came up with pet names for me, my wife, and our youngest son. I became known as "Hefty," a dubious name for the biggest hamburger on the menu; Jan took on the name of "Hot Fudge" in honor of her take-home request; and Rob, still a pre-teen, got to go along as "French Fry." So, around and around we went, honking our way through the campus and over the hill. When the caravan arrived at Herfy's, I was again escorted through a phalanx of students into a reserved spot at the head of the table. After our burgers, fries, and shakes, a riotous program began. Always in good taste, they poked fun at each other just like a Toastmaster's roast. Then, to cap off the evening, the students assembled a Rube Goldberg-type trophy to present to me. Bits and pieces of old sports trophies were hinged together along with the name "Hefty" and, when presented, it signaled another round of good-natured cheers for the old man.

Herfy Runs went on for the last six or seven years of our administration. When we left in 1982, a side room in the basement displayed all of the trophies from those years. As you would expect, the fourth-floor Ashton men had to outdo their predecessors every year by increasing the size of the trophy. The first one is about eighteen inches high and the last one stands all of five feet tall, a rag-tag collection of trophies standing one upon the other. Yet, this final trophy represents the last, best, and funniest of the Herfy Runs.

When the men of fourth-floor Ashton heard about my resignation from the presidency at Seattle Pacific University to move to Asbury Theological Seminary, they decided to make this last Herfy Run with me one to be remembered. At least ten cars made up the caravan and every car carried four or more students. As before, we heard their honks as they arrived at the President's home, answered the doorbell, walked through their outstretched arms, and took our place in the lead car for the procession. Many honks later I thought that they might have overdone it for the neighborhood, but who was I to complain? Finally, after going round and round Queen Anne Hill, we surfaced on Interbay at Herfy's. Everything went as planned except for an extra push on the finality of this event. I received my five-foot trophy, responded with a slapstick speech about the grandeur of this moment, followed with thanks from "Hot Fudge" and "French Fry" and then followed the escort back out to the lead car for the caravan. Another dizzy trip of twists and turns with honking horns took us back up Queen Anne Hill and to the campus of Seattle Pacific University. After one last blast around the campus, we arrived in front of Hillford House, only to be greeted by three or four squad cars with flashing blue lights. As we came to a stop, we heard a voice from a bullhorn commanding us to stop and stay in our cars. Our driver pulled up in front of the President's home and sat there, waiting for our next order from the police. I, however, got out of the car and went over the squad car parked immediately in front of our home. His window was half way down so I poked my head halfway in and said, "It's OK officer. I am the President." The window jerked up, almost taking my head off and the bullhorn blared, "I don't care *who* you are! *Get back in the car or I will book you!*" What can you say? My presidential authority went down the tube as I sheepishly returned to the car and sat in the front seat while the cop wrote tickets for disturbing the peace on each of the drivers. For the students, it was all part of the party. They laughed as I stewed. After the tickets were written, I again challenged the officer with my presidential authority only to be rebuffed by a gruff, "Back off, or I will hold you for the obstruction of justice!"

The students came to my rescue. After getting their tickets for disturbing the peace along with orders to pay the fine or appear in court, their own sense of justice took over. Like practiced attorneys, they rallied their troops, developed their case, and overwhelmed the judge with their complaint against a prejudicial cop who failed to attend the hearing. With a laugh of his own, the judge told the students to "Keep it down" on the Herfy's Run, threw the case out of court, and rebuked the police officer. The amateur attorneys won the day and vindicated my presidency. Today, when alumni reunions are held for the classes of that era, the story is sure to be retold. The punch line is a laugh, "And McKenna almost lost his head when the cop rolled up the window." Never underestimate the power of students motivated by a sense of justice.

Chapter 14

The Rabbit That Played a Grand Piano

"What monstrous absurdities and paradoxes have
resisted whole batteries of serious arguments,
and then crumbled swiftly into dust before the
ringing death-knell of laughter."

—Agnes Repplier

A RABBIT COMPLICATED our move across the country from Seattle, Washington, to Wilmore, Kentucky. Just a couple of months before we made our decision that I should accept the presidency of Asbury Theological Seminary, we bought a new, four-door Volkswagen Rabbit as Janet's car for shopping and chauffeuring Rob to school. The car was too small to drive 2500 miles across the country so we decided to ship it along with our furniture in the moving van. Little did we know at the time that a car with a German name was taboo in Kentucky even though it was assembled in Pennsylvania.

When the van arrived at the President's home in Wilmore, the unloading began with the driver directing the job and local hired hands doing the work. To accommodate the Rabbit and our furniture, the inside of the trailer had been turned into a double-decker with steel beams across the middle creating the second story. The Rabbit rode on the first level with our baby grand piano immediately above. The prized piano, my gift to Jan on our twenty-fifth wedding anniversary, was unloaded first.

For moving, the three legs of the piano had been taken off, so the workers had to carry the body of the instrument into the living room and then re-install the legs. I watched as two men held up one side of the piano so that the first leg could be screwed on. Then, they did the same for the second leg. With a heart-rending crunch, the piano crashed to floor. They had failed to secure the first leg so that all of the weight of the piano tore screws from the wood and buckled the veneer on the exquisitely shaped and lacquered side. Extensive damage would require a master workman to restore the piano.

While still recovering from this shock, the steel beams of the second floor over the Rabbit were removed and the car driven down the ramp. Another crunching sight greeted us. Sometime during transit, the steel beams had fallen on the Rabbit and left two deep creases into the roof of the brand new car with internal damage as well. By now, we were convinced that we were jinxed. Major insurance claims on two of our most expensive possessions had to filed and, in the case of the piano, we doubted that the veneer could ever be restored.

Once the rest of our furniture and goods were unloaded, we took the second stop in relocation: getting dinner for the family before all of the pots and pans are unpacked. Jan took the crinkled Rabbit to the only grocery in town, Fitch's IGA, a store that we knew from our student days as an institution in the community. When my wife arrived home, she couldn't contain her laughter. First, before stopping at Fitch's, she had driven down Main Street to renew her acquaintance with the block of stores that made up downtown. She said, "When I almost ran over a chicken crossing the street, I knew that I was back in Wilmore." But then Jan reported on her experience at the grocery story: "When I got to the checkout counter and introduced myself, John Fitch welcomed me to town and then consoled me, 'I am so sorry to hear that your grand piano fell and crushed your rabbit.'" Our shock level took another jump. In less than a few hours after our arrival detailed word had passed through the village grapevine and come out on the end with a juicy, but fallacious word of gossip.

Jan told John Fitch the whole story and they laughed together, but what a lesson. In the urban world of Seattle no one knows your business and few really care, but in the village of Wilmore everyone knows your business and most of them really care. Jan's genuine love for people and her joyful spirit quickly disarmed those who might have been suspicious of the President's wife. As for me, I admit that I remained wary of a rumor mill that could make or break you. In defense, I frequently asked the question, "Have you heard the story of the rabbit and the grand piano?" Truth proved funnier than fiction.

Chapter 15

The Little Piggy That Went to Missions

"Laugh, and the world laughs with you . . ."

—Ella Wheeler Wilcox

JULIAN CLAUDIUS MCPHEETERS tops my all-time list of unforgettable characters. He was my president during my student days at Asbury Theological Seminary. At that time, we seldom saw him because he was always on the road, preaching, teaching, and making friends for the Seminary. Yet, legend followed in his footsteps. As the second President of the Seminary, he had come from the position of senior pastor of Glide Memorial Methodist Church, located right in the Tenderloin District of San Francisco. From that pulpit he had taken to the streets with ministries of recovery for the prostitutes who walked those streets and for the poor and homeless who slept on the steps of the majestic church. From that pulpit, he had launched a national radio ministry, a devotional magazine, a summer camp in the Redwoods, and a thrust for world missions that echoed around the globe. Dr. McPheeters brought that reputation to the presidency of Asbury Theological Seminary in 1947. Although he was a little man in physical stature, he had a voice made for field preaching, so sonorous and enthusiastic that everyone got caught up in the sidewalk conversations as well as his preaching and his prayers.

Dr. McPheeters and I reconnected in 1982, the year that I was elected President of Asbury. He had retired in 1962, but still served with the title of President Emeritus. His zest for life never waned. At the age of seventy-three he had taken up water skiing, and to celebrate his eighty-ninth year he skied slalom for twenty miles. As part of his devotions to start the day, he went through a full schedule of weight-lifting, push-ups, stretches, and squats. In fact, at the age of ninety he held a physical fitness session for alumni pastors who attended the annual Minister's Conference, showing them his exercises while reminding them that physical and spiritual health go hand in hand.

I also heard the story about Dr. McPheeters' greeting for the dawn of every new day. Rising at 4 or 5 a.m. he threw back the curtains and shouted, *"This is the day that the Lord has made! Let us rejoice and be glad in it!"* Then he went to knees and stayed there until he had circled the world. On one of his trips representing the seminary, he took a faculty member with him. To save costs, they roomed together. True to form, on the first morning of their trip, Dr. McPheeters rose, threw back the curtains, and shouted his praise for the new day. The sleepy faculty member put up with early morning wake-ups for a couple of days and then asked his President if he would tone it down a bit so that he could get his sleep. Always compliant, Dr. McPheeters agreed. The next morning the faculty member heard him slip out of bed, go to the window, ease back the curtains, and whisper to the dawn, *"This is the day that the Lord has made, let us rejoice and be glad in it!"*

On the day of my election as President, I received two phone calls. The first one took all of the glow off my election. A wealthy but easily disgruntled trustee called me to say that he had resigned from the Board and withdrawn his gifts because I was not a member of the United Methodist Church. The second call came in the evening from Dr. McPheeters. We were out at the time so he left the message to call back through Operator 6 when we returned home. First thing the next morning, I placed the call. Dr. McPheeters' son, Chilton, answered the phone and said that his father was still in his devotions but would see if he could come to the phone. A couple minutes passed while Operator 6 and I waited. In the midst of our chat, a voice boomed over the phone, *"This is the day that the Lord has made! Let us rejoice and be glad in it! Good morning, David!"* Operator 6 could hardly contain herself with laughter and even forgot her responsibility to ask, "Will you accept the charges?" A stream of excited words followed as Dr. McPheeters continued, "David, I have just been praying for you, Janet, and your young son, Rob. Does he water-ski? I've got my boat at Dale Hollow ready to go." From there, he welcomed us to the seminary, assured us of his prayers, pledged his support, and told us that God had given him the promise that the needs of the seminary would be met.

When we arrived at the seminary, Dr. McPheeters was one of the first ones to visit my office. He popped in, spoke a word of encouragement, showed the plane tickets for his next trip, said a sentence prayer, and invited me to lunch with him the next day at the Springs Restaurant in Lexington, his favorite spot that featured the famous Kentucky Hot Brown (a combination of bacon, turkey, tomatoes, and cheese sauce on toast). Right on time the next day, he pulled up at the office in his brand new Chrysler Imperial. Dr. McPheeters had the reputation for changing Chrysler Imperials every year, but this one was different than the new one I had seen him driving a couple of days earlier. As we left the campus, he explained that earlier in the week he had had a fender bender with his other car. When he took it in for repairs, they said that it would take two weeks to fix it. Not willing to wait, Dr. McPheeters pointed out to the new car lot and said, "Then, trade me for that one." Whatever the cost, he had no time to waste.

Our entrance to the Springs Restaurant proved to be an event in itself. Dr. McPheeters' overwhelming presence swept over the large, open dining room and waitresses stopped their work to say "Hello" to their friend. The hostess seated us at a table for two against a lacquered plywood wall in full view of all of the diners, including a large table of twelve elderly men presided over by Happy Chandler, former Governor of Kentucky and U.S. Baseball Commissioner. Our waitress greeted Dr. McPheeters with a word of thanks for his prayers when she was sick. Of course, my host insisted that I become acquainted with the Kentucky Hot Brown. While waiting for our order, Dr. McPheeter's opened the conversation with the question, "Have I ever told you the story of the missionary hog?"

"No, you haven't. Tell me."

As if on cue, Dr. McPheeters' eyes widened and his voice raised a notch as he said, "Let me tell you. When I was the pastor of Lizzie Glide Memorial in the Bay Area, I drove over to Modesto to visit Mrs. Freitas, a wonderful Christian lady who supported our ministries."

"Yes," I interrupted, "She was my sponsor when I was a seminary student."

"Of course, of course. . . . Well, I was driving down the highway to her farm and following a pickup truck with a young hog standing in the back. Must be that the driver hit a bump in the road because I saw the hog fly through the air, out of the pickup, and land on the highway in front of me. I hit the brakes and barely missed the hog laying in the road."

With each excited word and animated gesture, Dr. McPheeters' voice rose another decibel and bounced off the plywood wall with an echo across the room. A sideward glance showed me that everyone was looking our way with a look of amusement. Dr. McPheeters, however, was so lost in his story that he raced right on.

"I got out of the car and went over to check the hog. He was dazed but able to stand. What could I do?"

"Well, I decided to put the little hog in the car and see if I could catch the truck. So, I picked him up and put him in the backseat and started to drive. The hog popped up on his hind feet and looked out the wide window. Can you imagine the sight that drivers saw when they passed us on the road?"

Another glance at our captive audience caught sight of unbridled laughter. They were not laughing at us; they were laughing with us. Dr. McPheeters was on a roll.

"I drove as fast as I could to try and catch the pickup. But, whoever he was, he was gone. Now, what could I do? Coming into a small town, I stopped to ask a farmer if he could help me find the owner."

"No," the answer came back, "But you might let a local farmer raise the hog for you."

Dr. McPheeters said that he took his suggestion, dropped the little hog at a local farmer and went on his way. Months later, word came that the hog had grown to full size and was ready for slaughter. Dr. McPheeters said that he had another decision to make. "What would I do with a full-grown hog?"

The Kentucky Hot Brown arrived, but went untouched.

In fullest animation, my host told the whole restaurant, "I decided to sacrifice my hog for world missions. Each year, we set aside a special day for world missions in our church. Why not have a barbeque with my hog turning on a spit and a chef slicing off pork for our sandwiches?"

Another sideward glance showed all of the diners looking toward us in anticipation of the answer. Dr. McPheeters' sped on.

"Well, we did it. Everyone turned out and we raised more money for missions than ever before. That's why I call that pig my 'Missionary Hog!'"

Then, without a break from that peak of excitement, he glanced down, saw the Hot Kentucky Brown, and asked, "David, will you say the blessing?"

I dropped my head and uttered a short, soft-spoken prayer with the hope that my words did not bounce off the plywood wall. When I finished, Dr. McPheeters' loud "*Amen!*" echoed across the room. I looked up and saw that the diners had returned to their meals. A smooth and gratifying buzz filled in the room. After all, their meal had already been blessed by a great man who loved a good laugh.

Chapter 16

The Yankee in Colonel Sanders' Court

"The most wasted of all days is the one without laughter."

—e. e. cummings

TO MOVE FROM Seattle, Washington, to Wilmore, Kentucky is more than a change of location; it is a change of worlds. In 1982 I took my wife, Jan, and youngest son, Rob, from the presidency of Seattle Pacific University to leadership of Asbury Theological Seminary. After loading the van, we flew to Chicago, picked up a car and drove down Interstate 75 to Lexington, Kentucky, a sophisticated university city ten miles from Wilmore, the home of Asbury Theological Seminary and Asbury College. After traveling on the multiple lanes of Interstate 5, we entered a belt-way around Lexington until turning south on Harrodsburg Road, which winds through the picturesque land of thoroughbred horse farms noted for their Kentucky bluegrass and white-washed fences. Ten miles south of Lexington, Harrodsburg Road comes to a "Y" with Lexington Avenue veering south into Wilmore. To call the road an "avenue" at that time is a bit of hyperbole because it narrowed into a two-lane road without the forgiveness of shoulders on either side. I can still remember entering that road for the first time on our move back to Kentucky, feeling choked, and wondering if I had made a mistake by asking my wife and son to change worlds with me. Having been a student at Asbury Seminary, I also remembered the joke that passed from generation to generation of students: "Wilmore is not the end of the world, but you can see it from there." Local residents might not find it funny, but the fact is that Lexington Avenue, after passing through Wilmore, meanders down to the Kentucky River and High Bridge, once the highest railroad trestle over a navigable river in the United States. There, it dead-ends.

I love both Seattle and Wilmore, even though they are worlds apart:

- Seattle is an urban metropolis on the shores of Puget Sound; Wilmore is a rural village on the edge of Appalachia;
- Seattle is the most secular city in our nation; Wilmore is a buckle on the Bible Belt,
- Seattle thrives on the spirit of radical individualism; Wilmore is steeped in the history of Southern tradition;
- Seattle is known for heavy metal music and grungy dress; Wilmore prefers country gospel and cowboy boots;

- Seattle chugs on exotic coffee; Wilmore sips on sweetened ice tea;
- Seattle loves its salmon and oysters; Wilmore relishes its catfish and sweetbreads;
- Seattle is the home of the new rich and the world's richest man; Wilmore prides itself on old wealth and historical homes.

The list could go on and on. How can a Midwestern kid, bounced between Seattle and Wilmore, ever make the adjustment?

My change of worlds began with learning a new language. Our son, Rob, had to trade soccer for basketball when he transferred from a private Christian school in Seattle to a public high school in Kentucky. He made the team, but only as a reserve picking up splinters from the bench. Still, his games had priority on my presidential schedule. In the very first game, we watched the championship cheerleading squad go through their dance and tumbling routine. Rob was dating one of the cheerleaders and when she talked, we had to tune our ears to her Southern drawl. I assumed, however, that the language would smooth out when ten cheerleaders yelled together. I was wrong. When they led a cheer, we could not make a word that they were saying. Finally, I tried to see if I could decipher their yell phonetically. As best I could determine, they were saying, "Gey-at, they-at, tee-ap!" It didn't make sense until I asked Rob's girlfriend to speak the words very slowly for me. Now they came clear. The cheer was "Get that tip!" Once I tuned my ear to the fact that Kentuckians make two syllables out of one, I learned to interpret the Southern drawl.

Cultures are not without contradictions. Seattle, for instance, is one of the wealthiest cities with thousands of homeless sleeping on the streets. Despite its reputation for being the most secular city in the nation, it is also home for some of our fastest growing megachurches. Kentucky has its own extremes. With the wealth of its horse farms creating the highest capital income in the country, it also bears the discrepancy of the greatest gap between the rich and the poor. Equally puzzling is the fact that Lexington is the location for the University of Kentucky—a top-ranking national research university—and Wilmore is the site for two outstanding institutions of Christian higher education. Yet, in the midst of these centers for learning, there are Appalachian people who are either illiterate or dropouts from school as soon as the law allows.

Tragedy and comedy are often ill-fitting partners. I felt this impact when I encountered the contradiction between literacy and illiteracy just outside of Wilmore. Wal-Mart opened a new superstore in Nicholasville, just five miles from Wilmore. On my first visit I went looking for a popular novel that ranked at the top of the New York Times' best-selling books. As I walked in the door, an elderly greeter welcomed me and asked, "Can I help you?" "Yes," I answered, "Where is your book section?" She gave me one of those "Yankee, go home" looks and scoffed, "We don't got no books."

The grammar shocked me, but not as much as the realization that I was the president of a graduate school of theology claiming, "The world is our parish," in the midst of people who lacked the ABCs of learning. The next time that I met my friend, Don Soderquist—COO for Wal-Mart and Chair of the Board at John Brown University in Arkansas—I turned the story into a joke and chided him. Don's laugh had a grimace in it. Wal-Mart now has a wide selection of books, and maybe, just maybe, I had something to do with it.

Was the man in the clothing store a relative of the Wal-Mart greeter? Probably not, but he sure got revenge on me for making a joke about Kentuckians. In another cultural contradiction, Nicholasville had a clothing store of traditional and classic fashions for men. I loved to browse the place, buy a tie, and occasionally pick up a suit or sport coat. On one of those visits, I stood in front of the rack of men's suits next to a clerk who was helping out a bearded man in rough work clothes who seemed to be out of place. As I fingered the price tags, I heard the clerk recommend a navy blue suit for him. The retort was instant and surely for my benefit. He growled, "I don't wear no Yankee blue!" You can be sure that I moved quickly down the rack from blue to grey suits.

Southerners are like college presidents. We can laugh at ourselves, but it is not funny when others are laughing at us. I took my humor on the road from Wilmore to Atlanta where I spoke at a dinner for donors and prospective donors to the seminary. My choice of a joke came from a sign that I had seen in the window of a restaurant. It read,

> FREE GRITS
> You have to ask for them.
> We don't waste our grits on Yankees

I thought that the sign was hilarious and the joke set up my speech very well. Afterward, I learned otherwise. When I stood at the door saying goodbye to our dinner guests, a very sophisticated elderly woman came by. Her fur stole, bejeweled neck, and Kentucky Derby hat reminded me of someone who had just stepped out from the novel *Gone with the Wind*. With steely eyes looking right through me, she said, "Young man, your speech was good, but your jokes were not funny." I blubbered an apology, but it was too late. The lady was gone, taking with her whatever gift to the seminary she might have made. As she walked away, I vowed never again to violate the sensitivities of the culture in which I was called to lead.

Chapter 17

The Rainstorm and the Rebel's Revenge

> "Laughter gives us distance. It allows us to step back
> from an event, deal with it, and then move on."
>
> —Bob Newhart

IF YOU PUT those who laughed with me and those who laughed at me on a scale, the weight would probably tip toward those who laughed at me especially when I tell stories about our time in Kentucky. If so, I can assure my Southern readers that the last laugh is on me.

Asbury College (now University) and Asbury Seminary are sister flagships for Wesleyan higher education. At times in past history, their relationship has become more competitive than cooperative. I tried to decipher the reason in order to seek reconciliation. Because the two institutions shared an overlapping constituency for fund-raising, it was inevitable that we would step on each other's toes from time to time.

Deeper than dollars, the history of our relationship revealed headstrong personalities who clashed over theological and lifestyle issues as well as economics. For some reason, their conflicts became contagious and spread from generation to generation. As I have already noted, every attempt that was made to bury the hatchet but the handle stayed close to the surface.

In the final years of my presidency, one of my former students and a close friend—David Gyertson—was elected as President of Asbury College. David and I had a relationship that overrode history even though there were still those who found excuses to keep the conflict going. To signal the advent of a new day, David and I started out by inviting each other to speak in our respective chapels.

My turn came in the spring of 1993 when Kentucky was in full bloom and glistening after a refreshing rainstorm. I, too, felt fully energized by the thought of speaking again to undergraduate students as I had so many years earlier at Spring Arbor University and Seattle Pacific University. Fully prepared to give the speech without notes, I left my office looking my best, in a navy blue suit, white dress shirt, a Robert Talbot striped tie, and tasseled loafers. Of course, I carried my black leather Bible with the gold imprint of my name under my arm. Almost unconsciously, I started to cross Lexington Avenue, silently rehearsing my speech as I walked. Halfway across I looked up to see a puddle of water overflowing the curb and extending into the middle of the street. A pickup truck that had come out of nowhere was bearing down on me. Detouring quickly to the right, I avoided the main puddle, jumped over to the grassy median, and turned left again to

The Rainstorm and the Rebel's Revenge   95

get back on course. No sooner had I made it safely across than I heard the whooshing sound of the pickup hitting the water, sending a spray over my head and thoroughly soaking my left side, Bible and all. When I blinked my eyes opened, I saw the image of a rusty pickup truck cascading through the flood with the bearded driver in a CAT hat peering back at me with a toothless grin that spelled, "*Gotcha!*" True to form, his face was framed in the rear window with a gun in its rack and in the back of the pickup, a large, wolf-like dog stood sentinel over the proceedings. To make the picture complete, the back bumper had two obvious stickers, one showed the Confederate flag and the other read, "MADE IN AMERICA."

My anger paralyzed me. Then, I felt the water dripping down my left side into my shoe and I saw the soaked pages of my Bible. I needed to change clothes before going to the chapel but my bad habit of procrastination had caught up with me. When I left the office, I barely had time to walk to the chapel, meet the President, and take the platform. There was nothing to do but keep going with the hope that I would dry out on the way. After the opening hymn, prayer, and the President's introduction, I took the platform. Still feeling soaked, I told my story to the students. Obviously, I had a captive audience who laughed with me—until I drew the conclusion. Reaching back to the reputation of Seattle as a rain-soaked world, I told the story of the college president who was about to retire. When I asked him where he intended to live, he said, "I am going attach an umbrella to the hood of my car and start driving. When someone stops me, looks at the umbrella, and asks, "What's that?" I will get out and live there the rest of my life." Paraphrasing his story, I told the students, "When I retire I am going to get in a car and start driving. When I no longer see rusty pickups driven by CAT-hatted, bearded, and toothless drivers with gun racks in the rear window, a guard dog in the back, and bumpers stickers showing the Confederate flag and reading, 'MADE IN AMERICA,' I will stop there and spend the rest of my life."

It was supposed to be funny, but I divided the house. Like drawing a line in the sand, Southerners scowled while Northerners laughed. I had done it again. Some place out in the hills of Kentucky, there is a man who laughs and laughs when he tells the story of hitting the puddle and dousing some goody-goody preacher who was crossing the street. He is laughing at my expense, but now I can laugh with him. We are all products of our culture, and to assume that I am better than another is to draw the false conclusion that God plays favorites with me in the lead.

Chapter 18

The Saintly Rider on a Wayward Horse

> "Self depreciating humor can be a healthy reminder
> that we are not the center of the universe, that
> humility is our proper posture before our fellow
> humans as well as before almighty God."
>
> —C. S. Lewis

ASBURY THEOLOGICAL SEMINARY received a bequest from the estate of Ralph Waldo Beeson in 1990 that proved to be the largest single grant ever given to a freestanding seminary in American history. A president's dream came true when we were able to plan for a complete campus remodeling and envision the high technology of the first "smart campus" among graduate schools of theology. Both the plan and the vision came true when the project was completed in 1995, but not without some laughable moments that gave comic relief to our serious work.

Deep and vital roots in the Wesleyan theological tradition give Asbury Theological Seminary its mission and its spirit. Remembering the architect's adage, "We build our buildings and they build us," I saw the opportunity for keeping the tradition alive in the symbols we created in our new buildings and on the campus itself. To immerse ourselves in the spirit of Wesleyan history, my wife and I traveled to England and followed the trail of John Wesley as he led the revival that transformed his nation. Beginning at Wesley's home and chapel in London, we discovered an oil painting showing Wesley holding up a Bible in one hand and gesturing toward his hearers with the other. The caption on the brass plate read, "Offer them Christ," the very words that Wesley gave to Thomas Coke as he sailed for America with the assignment to bring Methodism to our shores. As we stood transfixed before the picture, I said, "We must duplicate that picture with a statue on campus so that each generation of students will be reminded of Wesley's message."

Back home, we engaged a sculptor who specialized in bronze to design the statue for a spot at the crosswalks of the campus where students would pass by everyday.

He accepted the commission and began his work. Months later, John Wesley appeared on campus just as we had seen in the painting on the staircase at his home. When the contractors erected the statue on the campus, however, it was so small that it appeared to sink into the ground and lose any impact upon its viewers. Too late, we learned that outdoor statues should be sculpted one and one-half life size. Wesley's statue was only life-size and he stood just 5 feet 4 inches tall. In desperation, I rushed into the gap by ordering the contractor to put him on

The Saintly Rider on a Wayward Horse 99

a pedestal of a round stone step ten or twelve inches from the floor of the patio. No impact. So, I ordered another step added to give more height to the statue. Still, no impact. One more step took us to the limit, but at least Wesley stood above the heads of the students passing by. We turned our boner into a laugh by introducing Wesley at the unveiling as a little man who became a giant when he climbed the steps of the market cross in the market squares of English towns, preached from the Word, stretched out his hands to the millers and the miners, and offered them Christ.

President Harry Truman was once asked, "What do you do when you make a bad decision?" Showing his crusty character, he spat back, "I make another." This is what I did after recovering from the fiasco of the statue of John Wesley.

As the next step in preserving the history of the seminary by campus symbols, we proposed a statue of Francis Asbury, the father of American Methodism, on horseback at the entry to the college and seminary campuses that are named after him. The site on Lexington Avenue had the ring of history because Asbury himself had ridden down that road back in the early 1900s on his way to the Wilmore camp meeting when Kentucky was still part of the Eastern frontier. No mistake this time. We ordered the sculptor to make sure that the statue was one and one-half times the life-size of Asbury and his horse.

Our intention was to make this magnificent bronze sculpture a point of pride for both the college and the seminary. In fact, we got permission from the college to duplicate the desk-sized sculpture of Asbury and his horse that had been commissioned for its centennial anniversary. The first of these sculptures had been presented to President Ronald Reagan who proudly displayed it on the credenza behind his desk in the Oval Office. In my mind's eye, I envisioned this stately symbol welcoming visitors to the village and setting the tone for both campuses.

Months later, we were informed that the statue was ready for placement. The sculptor himself would direct the work. When the massive piece came, we were awed. One and one-half life size proved the point. The statue was larger than life and bigger than we expected. I saw it standing on the corner facing into the intersection with Asbury riding tall over the slightly turned head of the horse. When I proposed that position, the sculptor's voice took on an edge of anger. "No," he said, "There is only one way to place a rider on horseback. It must be sideways, showing the full statue, with the horse's head pointing northeast." I pressed my case, but only to hear the sculptor's retort, "Either we do it my way or we do not do it all!"

And so the statue of our founder, Francis Asbury, stands broadside to the intersection so that visitors see the full view of horse and rider as they approach the entrances to the college and seminary. Lexington Avenue, however, is more than the road down which Francis Asbury traveled 200 years ago. It is also the dividing line between college and seminary campuses. Even though they are sister institutions with common Wesleyan roots, there have been moments in the past when cooperation got lost in personalized conflicts, usually under the cover of theological differences. An observer of one of those conflicts commented, "Lexington Avenue dividing the college and the seminary is as wide as the Jordan River."

Memories of those conflicts came to the surface as soon as Francis Asbury and his horse were in place. Allegedly, someone "across the street" noted that the rear end of the horse pointed toward the college! Word spread quickly that I had deliberately placed the horse in that position to let the college know what I thought about them. Horrors! No one knew the story of my struggle to point the horse's head out to the street and the rear end toward the seminary campus. People on both sides of the street now laugh at the idea of a conspiracy and are reaching out to each other with open arms. Francis Asbury would be the first to concur. His circuit-riding ministry is credited with helping to heal the breach between the Eastern seaboard and the Western frontier in the nineteenth century so that we can truly say that we are "One nation under God." Nothing would please him more than to know that the two institutions that bear his name are "One family under God."

Chapter 19

The Smart Campus That Sprung a Leak

> "At the height of laughter, the universe is flung into a kaleidoscope of new possibilities."
>
> —Jean Houston

HI-TOUCH MET HI-TECH in our dream for the future of Asbury Theological Seminary. With the deep roots of our Wesleyan tradition represented in the statues of John Wesley and Francis Asbury gracing the campus, we also envisioned branches of ministry reaching out to every corner of our world parish. The Beeson bequest made that dream a possibility with resources that enabled Asbury to become the first "smart campus" among theological seminaries with all of the latest technology for research, teaching, and communication by satellite around the world. For instance, John Wesley's world could again be seen in the architecture of a chapel that was modeled after Wesley's first church, called "New Room," in Bristol, England. My wife and I stood in awe of the creative design for the church when we visited New Room on a self-guided tour of Wesley's world. The church is hexagonal in shape with seating that gives the congregation a sense of participation by proximity to the preacher and each other. Backed by a massive organ, a seven-foot pulpit raises the preacher to eye level with the people in the surrounding balcony. High above the sanctuary is an inverted copula, also hexagonal in shape, dropping down from the ceiling with windows on each side so that John Wesley could observe the preacher in the pulpit from one side and the response of the congregation on the other. Rooms above the sanctuary included sleeping rooms for John and Charles Wesley, study rooms for scholars, and seminar rooms for teaching homiletics to the student preachers who occupied the sanctuary pulpit.

Jan and I brought home that design for the new preaching chapel on the campus. Hexagonal in shape, seating designed to bring the congregation into a sense of community, a high platform with a line of vision to the balcony, a magnificent organ, and an eight-sided cove in the ceiling with video cameras pointing both ways to view the preacher and the response of the people. When finished, it would be a high-tech version of New Room, Bristol.

Construction began with a deep, gaping hole dug for the pilings that would go into the quarry stone of the Appalachian area. At the depth specified on the blueprints, however, the shovels uncovered one of the underground caves that honeycomb through Kentucky. This cave was as big as a two-car garage and forewarned the workers that there were probably adjoining caves in the area. We had no choice but to dig deeper at an added cost of over $200,000. Once below the caves the diggers ran into a water table gushing from artesian wells. Our problems mounted as the waters rose to fill the huge hole that had already been dug for the new chapel. The next morning, I got a call from Vice-President Eugene Lintemuth, resident manager of the construction, to hurry down to the campus before the construction workers arrived. His attempt to sound serious was betrayed by a chuckle. Arriving on the campus a couple of minutes later, Vice-President Lintemuth took me to the second floor of the library that overlooked the construction site. As we looked down, we saw water filling the hole and overflowing the banks, but the more commanding sight was a large, hand painted sign on top of the small mountain of dirt that stood between us and the water. It read, "LAKE MCKENNA." No wonder my Vice-President could not hide his chuckle. The laugh was on me and everyone on campus shared his chuckle. Because I had worked so hard at getting super-serious seminarians to lighten up and sound a note of joy, I decided that it was a sign of success, even if it had a barb in it. If we cannot laugh at ourselves when others laugh at us, we lose all perspective and become self-pitying grumps. I take "LAKE MCKENNA" as a humorous compliment, a breakthrough among seminary students who sometimes tended to take themselves too seriously, even if it came at my expense.

The story is not over. Like the Lady of the Lake rising out of the sea, a chapel rose out of the waters and stands today as a tribute to Wesley's New Room at Bristol. At the time of our retirement in 1994 the Board of Trustees at Asbury Theological Seminary named the chapel after my wife and me. Better yet, Vice-President Lintemuth came up with the idea of tapping the artesian wells to provide an inexhaustible source of water for irrigating the seminary lawns. Today, when Kentucky bluegrass burns to brown in the summer drought, Asbury's campus is a lush green. The cool, clear waters that created Lake McKenna are still flowing.

Chapter 20

The Ghost in the Choir Loft

"Imagination was given to man to compensate
him for what he is not;
a sense of humor to console him for what he is."

—Francis Bacon

OH, THAT WE could see ourselves as others see us. During my career as a college president I gained the notorious reputation for always being late for meetings. One outspoken critic said, "McKenna comes late so that he can draw attention to himself." That hurts. Even though Sheila Lovell, my Executive Assistant, tried to keep me on schedule, I usually rushed into meetings either late or at the last minute. I reject, however, the idea that it was an attention-getting device. Chalk it up to the bad habit of trying to get one more thing done before moving on to the next item on my schedule. Whether driven by ego or agenda, my tendency for late arrivals produced the laugh of all laughs in my thirty-three years as a leader.

As President of Asbury Theological Seminary, I frequently received invitations to preach in local churches. Because of my weekday travel schedule, however, I had to be selective in my decisions. If the invitation came from one of the key churches in our constituency, I gave it serious consideration. In one case, however, sentiment and persistence got the best of me. My secretary, Lois Mulcahey, asked if I would preach at Park United Methodist Church, her home church in Lexington, Kentucky. I kept deferring, but she persisted with the reminder that Park UMC was the home church for Bill Savage, a prominent banker in Lexington and long-time trustee of the seminary. Also, he and his wife, Dottie, were our close, personal friends. So, as my final ploy, I said that I would preach if Lois would sing. I thought that would put an end to the idea. Instead, she said, "Yes" and I was trapped. The pastor sent the invitation and I accepted.

Park United Methodist Church has the reputation of one of the grand old churches in Lexington. It stands on the corner of Woodland Avenue, right in the midst of history with the homes of Henry Clay and Mary Todd Lincoln nearby. Methodist tradition guided the worship with an organ, choir, formal order of service, and, of course, the preacher in a robe.

When Lois left the President's Office on Friday afternoon preceding the Sunday service, she left a manila folder on my desk with large, red letters handwritten on the front, "PARK UMC, 11 A.M. WORSHIP. BRING YOUR ROBE AND BE THERE NO LATER THAN 10:45 A.M." In this note, you can see that she knew me very well. Detailed instructions included the fact that I dare not forget to bring my powder blue academic gown from the University of Michigan with the blue and gold velvet on the sleeves designating my PhD. Equally important, I had be there at least fifteen minutes ahead of the service for final briefing and prayer with the pastor.

When Sunday came, I dutifully obeyed instructions. Hanging the doctoral gown in the car, my wife and I set out for Lexington at exactly 10:30 a.m. As usual, I was squeezing the time, but I felt sure that I could drive the ten or so miles from Wilmore to the south side of Lexington on a quiet Sunday morning. My calculations proved right. At precisely 10:44 a.m. I pulled in front of the United Methodist Church with the intention of letting Jan drop me off at the door so that I could walk through the door exactly at the designated time. As I got out of the car, I saw the name of the church in bold letters, "Southern Hills United Methodist Church." Even though I had driven past this church hundreds of times on the way to downtown Lexington, I had never paid attention to the name. Precisely at the right time, we were at the wrong church!

True to my macho self, I did not stop to ask directions. Instead, I thought, "Oh, now I remember. Park Church is over on East High Street, just north of the university." Away we went, following my nose, because I still wasn't quite sure how to get there. Another revelation unnerved me when we arrived at the center of town only to remember that High Street was one-way street going west rather than east. Now, I had to drive a block past our street and find our way back to the point where it became a two-way street again.

By now, the witching hour of 11 a.m. had arrived. Someplace out there, a secretary, a pastor, a choir, and a congregation awaited a delinquent guest preacher. Right then, we surfaced from a side street on to East High and saw the stately old church in front of us. To add to my assurance, I spotted a pink Cadillac parked at the curb and exclaimed, "This is it. There is Bill and Dottie's Cadillac." Seeing no place to park on the street, I turned into the lot at the back of the church and, in desperation, took the only spot left. Even though it was marked "Reserved for the Handicapped" I felt as though I qualified. Grabbing my robe, I ran from the car, through the door, and into a room with double doors opening to the sanctuary and stairs leading to the choir loft. The worship service was well underway so I stripped off my suit coat, put on my robe, and peeked through the double doors. I saw the pastor standing at the pulpit and asking the congregation to stand for prayer. "Great," I thought, "I can sneak in from the back when everyone has their eyes closed and be there when the prayer is finished." Racing up the stairs to the choir loft, I stepped out and joined the choir. Soprano eyes opened and alto heads turned to see a stranger in power blue doctoral garb standing out like a speckled bird against their bright red choir robes. To say the least, they were baffled. For me, however, I looked down the steps of the choir loft in search for an opening to the pulpit. Alas, there was none. The choir was boxed in by a wooden railing that separated them from the preaching platform. There was no point of entry.

A new note of desperation took over as I spun around, went back through the door, down the stairs, and into the robing room with the double doors leading to the sanctuary. Putting my ear to the door, I heard the pastor continuing to pray so I hesitated just long enough to spot the bulletin for the service on a table next to the doors. Picking one up, I opened it to see where I fit into the program.

My name wasn't there.

"Someone made a mistake," I thought. But then, I glanced at the top of the program and saw the name, "WOODLAND

CHRISTIAN CHURCH." Another wave of panic swept over me as I stripped off the gown, grabbed my suitcoat, and headed for the front door to rescue Jan from the congregation. My watch now showed 11:16 a.m. As I rushed through the front door of the church I met Jan rushing out. After being seated by the usher, she too looked at the program and realized that we were still in the wrong church. Finally, then, I asked the usher for directions to Park United Methodist Church. "Sure," he answered, "It's just a block down the street."

All systems went into reverse as we ran to the car, drove out, and spotted our destination on the next corner ahead of us. Out in front of the church, a solitary figure paced up and down. It was Lois, my secretary, in total despair because I had ruined her day. Once again, I parked illegally, grabbed the robe, and ran through the doors to the pastor's study. By now, he was stalling for time, extending announcements, and adding an extra verse on the hymn. Still, he graciously welcomed me to the pulpit. Lois then courageously sang her song and my turn came. As I told my story, it is an understatement to say that those staid old Methodist traditionalists were rolling in the aisle. By the time I got to the sermon, they were all mine.

While Methodists roared with laughter, I can imagine the conversation of the choir members at Woodland Christian Church after the service:

"Did you see that weird guy in the blue robe standing in the bass section?"

"Yes, I thought that I was seeing things."

"Maybe it was a ghost"

"Like a former pastor coming back to haunt us?"

"How did he disappear so quickly?"

"Did you ask the pastor?"

"Yes. He thought that I was crazy."

As for me, my dreams are haunted by the thought, "What would have happened if I had walked through the doors, up the stairs, and crossed the platform? Can you imagine the look on the pastor's face when I appeared? What would he have said after I introduced myself as the guest preacher? What would I have done standing in front of the whole congregation, red-faced, and ready to run? Could I laugh at myself when everyone was laughing at me?

As for God, he must have been laughing too, but not without some sympathy for his procrastinating preacher. True to his nature and with his good sense of humor, he again gave the gift of grace to rescue me from myself and save me from my most embarrassing moment.

As for the pastor of Woodland Christian Church, he has no idea what happened. You can be sure that I will never be the one to tell him.

Chapter 21

The Bad Money in a Good Book

> "You don't stop laughing because you grow old; you grow old because you stop laughing."
>
> —Michael Pritchard

SOME PEOPLE ARE accident-prone. I am incident-prone. As my wife Jan says, "If there is a bone in the salmon or a pit in the cherry, Dave always gets it." Perhaps this will explain an incident that could only happen to me at the age of eighty while on exile from our condo on the shores of Lake Washington.

On December 9, 2009, the temperature dropped in Seattle to a record low. We took it in our stride until December 10. At 2:10 p.m., Jan and I had just taken the first bite out of our tuna fish sandwich when the fire alarm blared in our ears. I ran out of our condo, into the center court, and looked up through the open well to the third-floor condo above us. A cascading waterfall poured out of the walls and down three floors, swamping each condo on the way. I called to Jan, "Oh, our neighbors are trouble." She answered with a yell, "Help! It's coming through the ceiling in the closet." Spinning on the spot, I ran back into our condo, through the master bedroom, and saw a veritable gusher of water coming from a hole in the ceiling where a florescent fixture had been blown from its moorings and had crashed to the floor. Our clothes were drenched and water was flowing out from under the baseboards to flood the carpets and the wood flooring. A frantic attempt at moping and swooshing proved futile. Everything was ruined by the water and our condo now qualified as a disaster area. Within a short time, our furniture and all of our belongings, including every book in my personal library, were lifted out of the water to be packed up and carted off to storage.

We became exiles from our home. After a short stint at the Residence Inn, we were relocated in an apartment in the Seattle area, presumably for a period of three or four months. Although it was not home, we were quite comfortable in an urban setting of high-rise buildings in proximity to the public library, across the street, and a shopping mall, just three blocks away. I told my friends that we were ideally located because I am an incurable bibliophile who loves to read while Jan is a cured buyer who loves to look.

According to Garrison Keillor, Seattle is known as a city with more dogs than Christians. True or not, I didn't expect much from my first visit to the public library in our secular city. The Religion section proved to be weak, especially in areas of special interest, such as Christian Theology and Biblical Studies. To my surprise, however, I found that most of the highly recommended books on Christian Living and

Inspiration had long wait lists on them. Empty handed, I returned home.

A couple of days later, *Christianity Today* came out with its 2010 Book Awards. In the category of Christianity and Culture, the Award of Merit went to *American Babylon: Notes of a Christian Exile*, written by my friend, Richard John Neuhaus, before his death in January 2009. I had to get the book and read it right away, but hesitated buying it because my temporary bookshelf was already piling up with volumes that we would have to move back home. Also, with my Scotch blood flowing, I decided to take a chance and see if our public library had it. To my delight, the card catalog had the reference and the visual shelf showed the book available. Up the stairs I went to the top floor and back into the stacks where you could feel the loneliness that is reserved for a rare book collection. High on the shelf I spotted the red lettered title *American Babylon*, pulled it down, and headed for the stairs to check it out. In the middle of my descent, my curiosity prompted me to open the book and check out the table of contents. When I did, the pages parted around a stack of dollars that had been neatly tucked like a centerfold into the middle of the book. On top, I spotted a five-dollar bill that promised more underneath. Looking around and seeing no one, I folded the money and put it in my pocket with the thought, "Jan will have to see this to believe it."

Then, caution checked in. *American Babylon* felt like a hot coal in my hands. If I took the book out, perpetrators of foul play might be able to identify me and seek revenge. So, with sleight of hand, I left it on table next to a check out screen and headed home. At the door to our rental apartment I called out, "Jan, come here. You won't believe this." I gave her the stack of bills and watched as she peeled them off one at a time. Two hundred-dollar bills appeared along with a couple fifties and more fives—a total to $325!

Jan looked at me and I looked at her. What in the world had I stumbled into? Who would put that amount of money in a book? Why was such an unlikely book as *American Babylon* chosen? How could I be the one to pick it up? Was it lost or part of a conspiracy? Had I innocently become involved in a felony? Right or wrong, I decided to keep the money until I found some answers.

Our family loves to play games. Whether a table game, lawn game, political guessing, or theological difference, they are always up to a challenge. So I exercised my paternal prerogative and made a game out of my dilemma. Emails went far and wide to kids and grandkids across the nation with the story and the question, "What would you do?" (Sorry. I failed to ask, "What would Jesus do?"). Answers came right back. Our youngest grandchildren, unspoiled by conflicting motives, simply said, "Give it back." At the next age level, word came, "Give it back and find out who checked out the book." Grown grandkids got a big kick out of my plight and proposed, "Take Grandma out for a romantic dinner." One even proposed, "Buy Mom the purse she always wanted."

When Tolstoy wrote, "Happy families are all alike; every unhappy family is unhappy in its own way" as the opening line for his novel *Anna Karenina*, he did not tell us what happy families have in common. Conventional answers include, "Happy families are all alike because they pray together" or "Happy families are all alike because they play together." From my own personal experience, I want to add, "Happy families are all alike because they love to make fun of Dad." Fathers and grandfathers will instantly understand when I ask, "Why is it that our kids and grandkids refuse to laugh at our jokes, but go hysterical when the joke is on us?" Some might claim that it is subtle rebellion against years of parental authority or revenge for the number of times father said, "That's *not* funny!" My answer is different. I believe that having a laugh at Dad's expense is a sign of a happy family. Let the opposite prove my point. Have you ever known an unhappy family where the kids enjoy poking fun at Dad? If they do, hatred rises, hurt deepens, and alienation accelerates. A happy family, however, is one in which mutual love and respect welcomes the sound of laughter, the creativity of playful pranks, and the gentle joshing with Dad as the favorite target.

Our children and grandchildren took full advantage of my plight. With glee, they began to write scenarios about the consequences of an ordained minister and university president finding bad money in a good book. Our attorney son-in-law, Ed Blews, wrote to warn, "This sounds like a drug sting. Don't touch it." Our psychologist son, Doug, added, "I didn't want to tell you, but $325 is the going rate for an ounce of marijuana in Seattle." Together, then, they envisioned a newspaper headline in the Seattle Times reading, "FORMER SEATTLE PACIFIC UNIVERSITY PRESIDENT CAUGHT IN DRUG STING." Their words cancelled whatever was left of my innocence and sparked the imagination of a family that loves to laugh at my expense.

On Saturday morning after my Friday night adventure, Doug and Suzanne—our youngest daughter—appeared at our home-in-exile across from the library with a *CSI* mindset to sleuth out the mystery. First, they explored all of the scenarios that might fit a crime. Were counterfeit bills being passed? Was the money marked to catch the culprit? Was a street gang involved in a drug transaction? Were undercover police setting up a sting operation? Was someone on the library staff involved? To dramatize the scene, Suzanne used a pencil to push the money around so that she would not leave telltale fingerprints of the bills. Doug then tried a smear test to see if the ink would run. When both of these tests produced no results, they decided to go over the library and see if there were any signs of a surveillance camera or a security guard that might suggest a sinister plot. About thirty minutes went by before they returned to say that no surveillance cameras were seen and no security guard passed by, but while they were heading up the stairs to the isolated stacks, they saw an anxious teen in baggy jeans, black T-shirt, and backward cap racing down the opposite staircase and out the door. They recommended against any kind of involvement. If it was drug transfer that failed, someone was going to get hurt.

The hot coals of mystery money flared into flame. Earlier questions came back. What do we do with it? Have I stumbled on to a drug ring that uses the library for its drops? What if I return the money and the story becomes public information? Will I open myself to intensive interrogation? None of these questions had a satisfactory answer.

Leave it to me. Perhaps for the first time in human history, I was dealing with the ethical issue of finding bad money in a good book. Rationalization began with memories from the past. When Billy Sunday was asked if he would accept "tainted" money, he answered, "The only tainted money I know is 'taint' enough." D. L. Moody got a similar challenge when he was asked if he would accept a contribution that had come to his ministry from gambling earnings. Sunday answered, "The devil has had it long enough. Let's see what the Lord can do with it."

With those edgy thoughts in mind, I decided that I would put the bad money to good use. Word came that a life-taking and soul-shattering earthquake had hit Haiti. Jan, who had served on a college missions trip to Haiti, had a special spot in her heart for the impoverished island and its people. My own heart became personally involved when word come that Jeanne Acheson-Munoz, managing editor for one of my books, had been crushed under the concrete of a collapsing building. We weighed the gift that we would make for Haiti relief and then added $325 from the money that I had found. Whether you agree or not, it was a way of using bad money for a good cause. Once again, we saw the triumph of the ludicrous and the truth that was stranger than fiction. What began as an intellectual quest turned into a laugh on me, became an ethical snarl, and ended up as a gift of mercy.

Oh yes, after scouting the book through a crack in the stacks for a week or so, I checked out *American Babylon: Confession of an Exile*. Irony of ironies, Father Richard John Neuhaus, Lutheran pastor turned Roman Catholic priest and a leading Christian ethicist, would surely have an opinion on my decision. After laughing at my plight and chiding me for turning an easy answer to a murky moral quandary, I can hear him shifting to his private voice and chuckling once again, "Don't tell anyone, but I rather like the idea of putting the bad money in my good book to its highest and best use."

Epilogue

The Joy of God's Good Pleasure

> "Joy is the simplest form of gratitude."
> —Reinhold Neibuhr

WHAT IS THE moral of the story? This ponderous question pressed itself upon me after I spoke at a banquet attended by alumni and friends of one of the universities were I served as president. As I prepared my speech, I decided that these people had heard me give enough serious speeches and sober sermons. So, I chose the topic, "The Laugh's on Me—Confessions of a College President." Some of the stories in this book made up the speech. As I unraveled experiences where I laughed at myself, my listeners seemed to join the fun at my expense. Then, as I drew to a close, I saw disappointment cloud their faces. They were waiting for the moral of the story and the point of the sermon. A couple of months later, after giving a serious speech to many of the same people, one friend who had attended the banquet complimented me and then added,

"We really needed to hear you speak like that." I felt as if he wanted me to redeem myself from trying to be funny. Or, was I the victim of the perception that a college president cannot be human, especially when it comes to laughing at himself?

After that experience, I am sure that you are asking, "Why then, would you write a whole book entitled *When God Laughs with Us: The Lighter Side of Leadership*?" In defense of my decision, I was first tempted to write a concluding chapter called, "The Moral of the Story." Multiple options opened up. To begin, I would have to defend myself against the dark philosophical pessimism of Friedrich Nietzsche, who said, "Perhaps I know best why it is man alone who laughs; he alone suffers so deeply that he had to invent laughter." Or, I would take on the despair of psychologist Gordon Allport, who concluded, "So many tangles in life are so ultimately hopeless that we have no appropriate sword other than laughter." Sigmund Freud would also deserve a response because he limited laughter to "an outlet for discharging psychic energy." Sooner or later, I would also have to contest the opinions of biblical scholars who find no room for a good laugh in Scripture or the conclusions of Christian theologians such as Augustine and John Wesley who saw laughter as either meaningless or sinful. All of these negative approaches leave me asking, "Is a good laugh anything more than an escape for suffering, a weapon against hopelessness, a cathartic for relief of tension, or a sure sign of sinfulness?" Surely, there is something missing.

Lifting my sights, I could have made a strong case for a good laugh, especially at oneself, as proof of self-awareness and humility. When the virtues of great leadership are cited, humility is invariably high on the list. Yet, a leader who claims to be humble falls into the trap of the Dominican monk who contended, "When it comes to learning, Jesuits are number one; and when it comes to piety, nobody can beat the Franciscans; but when it comes to humility, we're tops!" A full book could be written on the word *humus*, the biblical term meaning the "dust of the earth" from which God created us. From the same root word, we get "humanity," "humility," and "humor." The connection cannot be denied. When we remember that we are the dust of the earth, any show of arrogance is a vain attempt to be like God and a good laugh at ourselves is the antidote for idolatry. If push came to shove, I could even turn the 4-H connection among humus, humanity, humor, and humility into evidence of spiritual maturity.

After considering all of these defensive options, I rejected all of them and chose to write because laughing is good for laughing's sake. In the mind-boggling film *Man on Wire*, I find my champion. Philippe Petit is the man who walked on a tightrope back and forth eight times between the twin towers of the World Trade Center and even dared to lie down and "dialogue with a seagull" while suspended in space. After his arrest brought him international notoriety, Philippe said the he heard only one question repeated in every interview, "Why? Why? Why?" Sent to a psychiatrist, who asked the question once again as a test of his sanity, Philippe left the doctor speechless by answering, "I dance at the top of the world and you ask me, 'Why?' There is no 'Why.'"

The truth strikes home. Do we have to answer "Why?" when we are creating a thing of beauty or laughing at the foibles in ourselves? A serious fault line runs through our culture and our character when we have to post an instrumental value or a utilitarian outcome for every motive and every action. We have already paid a high price for this flaw in a culture where art, music, drama, poetry, play, and worship have lost so much of their intrinsic worth. A good laugh is equally a creative act of intrinsic value. It needs no justification because it is good in itself.

So, here is my theology of laughter in a nutshell. When I wrote the *Communicator's Commentary on Job*, I followed the angry cries of an innocent man against God for his suffering, even when it bordered on blasphemy. After his alleged comforters have exhausted their repertoire calling for repentance and Job himself is recycling his arguments, God speaks to him out of the whirlwind, "Who is this that darkens my counsel with words without knowledge? Brace yourself like a man: I will question you and you will answer me" (Job 38:2). Two sets of questions follow. In the first set, God confronts Job with the awe-evoking reality of his power. Asking question after question, God sets the truth, beauty, and goodness of creation before Job. The argument is logical and the appeal is to reason. Job, who has counted on logic to carry his case, has no further defense. Before the power of God's truth, he shuts his mouth and succumbs to superior reason.

God has a second set of questions to ask Job. Taking him completely by surprise, God spins the yarn of the hippopotamus and the crocodile, creatures that are the epitome of the ludicrous and leading characters in the theater of the absurd. In starkest contrast with the logical power, goodness, and glory of creation that Job has just seen, the hippopotamus is ugly and useless; the crocodile is hostile and incorrigible. Why create such a waste? Never let it be said that God lacks a sense of humor. These ridiculous creatures are more than proof of God's almighty power. The ugly and useless hippopotamus is created for God's own good pleasure and the hostile and incorrigible crocodile exists by his own permission. Yet, as contradictory as they are, God ranks the hippopotamus as "first among [God's] ways" (Job 40:19) and the crocodile as "king over all that are proud" (Job 41:34). Logic shut the mouth of Job, but the ludicrous opens his eyes. With insight that can only come from an epiphany, Job confesses, "I have heard you with my ears, but now I see you with my eyes. I repent and bow my head in ashes." (42:5). For the first time, Job sees that he, too, is a creature of contradictions, a brother of the hippopotamus and crocodile, existing by the pleasure and the permission of God. The ludicrous has done what logic could not do. Logic showed Job the God of truth, but it took the ludicrous to show him the God of grace.

From Job's story, it is just short step from a good laugh in the Old Testament to a sense of joy in the New Testament. Think of joy as laughing from the inside out, independent of circumstances, rising out of love, and expressive of grace. Like Job, then, we see with our eyes the final promise of Christ when he says to his disciples, "I have told you this so that my joy be in you and that your joy may be complete" (John 15:11). The promise is ours.

I never stop telling the story. A secular humanist named Lewis Mayhew set the tone for my presidential leadership. After my election as President of Seattle Pacific University in 1968, I invited Dr. Mayhew, Professor of Higher Education at Stanford University, to spend a week on our campus and help us set the direction for the future. On Monday morning, he came to my office to outline the plan for the week. He introduced himself as a "secular humanist" and said that he had no idea what we meant when we claimed to be an "evangelical Christian college," but he vowed to find out. On Friday morning, he returned to my office to report his findings. He began this time by saying, "I am still not sure what you mean when you say that you are an evangelical Christian college, but I know one thing, 'If you are who you say are, this campus will be characterized by a note of joy.'"

Dr. Mayhew's words set the tone for my leadership from then on. Whether on or off campus, at home or broad, my one desire has been to have a spontaneous note of joy resonating through every phase of my life and work. This desire has included learning to laugh—at myself. So, as you have read the stories in this book, my hope is that you will join me in laughing from the inside out with a sense of joy. You will then understand why I sign everything I write:

With his Joy!

David L. McKenna

About the Author

David McKenna has served for more than fifty years in Christian higher education, including thirty-three years as a college, university, and seminary president. At Spring Arbor College (now University), he developed a junior college into a four-year Christian liberal arts college; at Seattle Pacific University, he led the transition from a four-year college to university status; and at Asbury Theological Seminary, he gained and guided the largest grant ever given in American history to a freestanding graduate school of theology. In 1994, he retired as President Emeritus of Asbury Theological Seminary to write, speak, and consult on subjects related to leadership in Christian higher education and ministry. In 2003, he retired as Chair Emeritus, Board of Trustees, Spring Arbor University.

McKenna holds a BA degree in History from Western Michigan University, a Master of Divinity from Asbury Theological Seminary, a Master of Arts in Counseling Psychology and a PhD in Higher Education from the University of Michigan. He has been awarded ten honorary doctorates, named a Paul Harris Fellow with Rotary International, and honored by Stanley Kresge's endowment for the David L. McKenna Christian Leaders Scholarship for business students at Seattle Pacific University.

McKenna's presidencies have been recognized at Seattle Pacific University by the David L. McKenna Hall for the School of Business; at Asbury Theological Seminary by the David and Janet McKenna Chapel; and at Spring Arbor University by the David and Janet Carillon Tower.

As an educational leader, he served as Founding Chair for the Christian College Consortium (parent organization of the Council of Christian Colleges & Universities) and Secretary for the National Association of Independent Colleges and Universities. In 1980, he was a finalist for Secretary of Education in the Reagan Cabinet.

As a religious leader ordained in the Free Methodist Church, McKenna has held positions as Vice-President of the World Methodist Council, Consulting Editor for *Christianity Today*, and a national radio commentator with the weekly signoff, "You have heard the thoughts and felt the heartbeat of David McKenna." In civic leadership, he chaired Governor Dan Evans' select committee to study gambling in the State of Washington and was honored as First Citizen of Seattle in 1976. McKenna is the author of thirty-one books that range across the fields of psychology, biblical commentary, leadership, history, and theology.

David and Janet McKenna celebrated their sixtieth wedding anniversary in 2010. They are parents of four children (Douglas, Debra, Suzanne, and Robert), twelve grandchildren, and one great-grandchild. A lakeside condo in Kirkland, Washington, is their home.

www.ingramcontent.com/pod-product-compliance
Lightning Source LLC
Chambersburg PA
CBHW020855160426
43192CB00007B/930